D0928030

WITHDRAWN

This book explores the way in which Schubert revolutionized the Lied, transforming folk song into art song through the mixture of dramatic and lyrical vocal genres. By introducing dramatic poetic and musical traits within solo song settings, he turned the Lied into a highly expressive musical medium capable of conveying the complexities and nuances of the new Romantic poetry. In so doing, he created an art form which attracted nearly every subsequent composer of the period.

Schubert's numerous dramatic songs have baffled critics from his day to our own. Their unusual stylistic characteristics – throughcomposed form, progressive tonal structures, declamatory vocal lines, illustrative accompaniments – fly in the face of traditional conceptions of the Lied. Dr. Hirsch's discussion and analyses of selected dramatic Lieder illuminate Schubert's compositional innovation.

Schubert's Dramatic Lieder

Schubert's Dramatic Lieder

MARJORIE WING HIRSCH, M.W.

Levine School of Music, Washington, D.C.

CAMBRIDGE
UNIVERSITY PRESS

MT125
Sch78so
HG15
c.2

Published by the Press Syndicate of the University of Cambridge
The Pitt Building, Trumpington Street, Cambridge CB2 1RP
40 West 20th Street, New York, NY 10011–4211, USA
10 Stamford Road, Oakleigh, Melbourne 3166, Australia

© Cambridge University Press 1993

First published 1993

Printed in Great Britain at the University Press, Cambridge

A catalogue record for this book is available from the British Library

Library of Congress cataloguing in publication data
Hirsch, Marjorie Wing.
Schubert's Dramatic Lieder / Marjorie Wing Hirsch.
p.   cm.
Includes bibliographical references and index.
ISBN 0 521 41820 8
1. Schubert, Franz, 1797–1828. Songs. 2. Songs–Analysis, appreciation. I. Title.
ML410.S3H57 1993
782.42168' 092–dc20   92–31440 CIP

ISBN 0 521 41820 8 hardback

THE LILA ACHESON WALLACE
LIBRARY
THE JUILLIARD SCHOOL
LINCOLN CENTER, N.Y. 10023

6/94/Add alan
SN

To Sarah and Joni

CONTENTS

ACKNOWLEDGMENTS

A number of people deserve special thanks for the help and support they have given me in this study. I am particularly grateful to Professor Reinhard Strohm, who showed tremendous enthusiasm for the project in its initial phase as a doctoral dissertation at Yale University and later in its revision. His penetrating insights into Schubert's texts and musical settings, as well as the unflagging energy and excitement with which he approaches his own scholarly work, have been a continuing source of inspiration. Professor Rufus Hallmark of Queens College, CUNY, played a critical role in helping me to reshape the study as a book. His many suggestions, like those of my dissertation readers Leon Plantinga, Claude Palisca, and Jane Stevens, have proved invaluable. Professors Jeffrey Kallberg and Gary Tomlinson of the University of Pennsylvania were very helpful in defining the project's scope in its earliest stages. I benefited greatly from discussions with both of them on the role of genre in interpretation. Charles Williams and Camilla Russell graciously assisted with certain translations. I offer special thanks to Penny Souster, Lucy Carolan, and Caroline Murray at Cambridge University Press and Seton Music Graphics Ltd for their able editing and production of the book. To my parents, parents-in-law, grandparents, sisters, and brother I am indebted for their continuous encouragement. My husband, Alan, lent his excellent editing skills to the project. I am extremely grateful for the innumerable improvements he made to the manuscript, as well as for his patience and good humor. My two daughters, Sarah and Joni, helped keep things in perspective and have made it all worthwhile.

Use of the following material is gratefully acknowledged:
Brief excerpts from *Schubert: Memoirs by His Friends*, ed. Otto Erich Deutsch, trans. Rosamond Ley and John Nowell (London: A. & C. Black and New York: Macmillan, 1958). Reprinted with permission of A. & C. Black.

English translation of the Cathedral scene from *Goethe's Faust*, Parts I and II, translated by Louis MacNeice. Copyright © 1951, 1954 by Frederick Louis MacNeice; renewed 1979 by Hedli MacNeice. Reprinted by permission of Oxford University Press, Inc. and Faber and Faber Limited.

English translations of two song texts, "Lullaby" (D527) and "The Diver" (D77). Reprinted with permission of Schirmer Books, a Division of

Acknowledgments

Macmillan, Inc., and Victor Gollancz Ltd. from *Schubert: The Complete Song Texts*, Richard Wigmore, Translator. Copyright © 1988 by Richard Wigmore.

NOTE ON PITCH DESIGNATION

The following system of pitch designation is used:

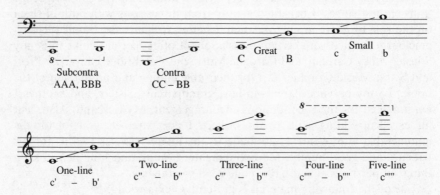

Introduction

On June 24, 1824, the Leipzig *Allgemeine musikalische Zeitung* published an anonymous review of eleven Schubert Lieder, Opp. 21–24. The author, a self-proclaimed spokesman for "fair-mindedness and modesty," decried the lack of order and restraint in Schubert's music:[1]

> Herr Fr[anz] S[chubert] does not write actual songs and has no desire to do so . . . but rather free vocal works, many so free, that one might perhaps call them caprices or fantasies. With this purpose in mind, the poems, mostly new but of greatly varying quality, are well chosen and their translation into music generally praiseworthy; the composer succeeds almost throughout in arranging the whole and each detail in accordance with the poet's idea. He is, however, much less successful in the execution, which tries to compensate for the lack of inner unity, order and regularity by eccentricities, barely or not at all motivated, and by often rather wild goings-on. With only these qualities [i.e., unity, order and regularity], admittedly, no artist's work can become a beautiful work of art. Without them, however, certainly only bizarre, grotesque things will result.

Schubert's strange tendency to modulate repeatedly within the compass of a song is deplorable, the writer continued, for "simplicity, repose, order, and clarity" are essential to a true masterwork.

This reviewer was hardly alone in his reaction to Schubert's compositional style. An 1826 letter to Schubert from the Artaria publishing firm shows that his music was widely perceived as eccentric and inaccessible:[2] "I must frankly confess to you that the peculiar, often ingenious, but occasionally also rather strange procedures of your mind's creations are not yet sufficiently and generally understood by our public."

The interpretive confusion surrounding numerous Schubert Lieder is reflected in the array of genre headings his contemporaries used to describe these works: freier Gesang, Kaprice, Phantasie, Tondichtung, durchkomponiertes Stück, Ballade, Kantate, and Szene. While there was no consensus on which terms were appropriate for particular songs, most writers agreed that Schubert "often, and sometimes very greatly, oversteps the genre in hand."[3] His songs frequently deviate from the conventions of traditional strophic Lieder. "In our opinion," stated one critic, "he is an actual song composer only at times."[4]

1

Introduction

To a large extent, Schubert's deviations from convention betray the influence of dramatic music. Both the poetic texts and the musical settings of many Lieder exhibit traits traditionally associated with dramatic vocal genres such as the operatic scene, concert scena, and melodrama. Used in reference to Lieder, the term "dramatic" does not merely signify a striking or forceful manner, although dramatic songs often have this characteristic. Rather, it implies an attempt to mimic the acts of impersonation and portrayal of action that take place on the theatrical or operatic stage. Schubert's dramatic songs depict one or several personae, often identifiable by name, engaged in a particular course of action. Between the first measure and the last, the personae experience a change of circumstance. Simple or complex, physical or psychological, something "happens."[5]

The dramatic quality of many Schubert Lieder was unsettling to early nineteenth-century music critics. One writer complained, "The musical representation sometimes encroaches, perhaps a little too much, upon the domain of the dramatic, for which Herr Schubert seems to us to have a special inclination."[6] Another likened Schubert's infusion of dramatic musical traits into traditional Lieder to "nations and warriors who, with the power of the sword, conquer peaceful countries and subsequently adopt the culture and language of the defeated."[7]

The critics' discomfort stemmed from Schubert's mixture of genres. This mixture operates on two levels. First, Schubert's Lied oeuvre includes traditional as well as non-traditional settings. Simple strophic folk songs stand side by side with powerful dramatic monologues. Secondly, many individual songs combine diverse traits, borrowed from lyrical and dramatic compositional models. "This kind of vocal music," concluded one early critic, "is too elaborate for genuine German song and too simple to be called dramatic."[8]

This book explores the crucial role of genre in the interpretation of Schubert's dramatic songs. Often bearing closer resemblance to dramatic vocal genres such as the operatic scene and melodrama than to folk song, many of these important works have been misunderstood and devalued. Their unusual stylistic characteristics fly in the face of traditional conceptions of the Lied. Examining Schubert's dramatic songs against the backdrop of genre, i.e., in relation to the musical traditions from which they emerged, offers new insight into individual works and shows their significance to his Lied repertoire as a whole.

While many writers have noted individual dramatic traits (e.g., recitative, throughcomposed form, progressive tonality) in Schubert's Lieder, the interrelationship among them has received little attention.[9] This study examines the network of characteristics that helps to identify various kinds of dramatic song. That investigation serves as a springboard for understanding how Schubert revolutionized the Lied. By combining elements of dramatic and traditional lyrical genres, he transformed the Lied into a highly expressive, flexible musical medium which could convey the complexities and nuances of the poetry. This was Schubert's great legacy to the nineteenth century.

Schubert's departure from traditional Lieder

The chasm separating dramatic songs from "actual song," as this term was understood in the 1820s, becomes strikingly evident through a comparison of the two Schubert Lieder published together in 1823 as Op. 24: "Gruppe aus dem Tartarus" and "Schlaflied." These songs, both composed in 1817, are among the eleven Lieder discussed in the *Allgemeine musikalische Zeitung* review quoted at the outset.[10] While the critic devotes no more than a few sentences to either work, he clearly recognizes that they have little in common.

"Gruppe aus dem Tartarus" (D583) is one of the most bizarre songs in Schubert's oeuvre.[11] This musical portrait of a group of damned souls in hell departs radically in subject, structure, and style from the traditional strophic Lied – the ideal song type in the minds of many early nineteenth-century writers. The dramatic nature of the setting, involving both textual and musical features, stands in sharp contrast to the "Volkstümlichkeit" characterizing traditional Lieder.

Schiller's poem draws its subject from Book VI of Virgil's *Aeneid*.[12] In this episode, Aeneas, guided by a prophetic Sibyl, travels to the Underworld in search of his father, Anchises. Before reaching the blissful Elysian fields where Anchises resides, they pass by the flaming fortress of Tartarus, from which emerges a dreadful din. In response to Aeneas' fearful queries, the Sibyl describes in ghastly detail torments suffered there by those who dared to rival the gods.

Schiller's poem compresses the Tartarus episode into three stanzas of four, six, and four lines, respectively:

Gruppe aus dem Tartarus (translation on p. 139)

Horch – wie Murmeln des empörten Meeres,
Wie durch hohler Felsen Becken weint ein Bach,
Stöhnt dort dumpfigtief ein schweres, leeres,
    Qualerpreßtes Ach!

Schmerz verzerret
Ihr Gesicht, Verzweiflung sperret
    Ihren Rachen fluchend auf.
Hohl sind ihre Augen – ihre Blicke
Spähen bang nach des Cocytus Brücke,
    Folgen thränend seinem Trauerlauf.

Fragen sich einander ängstlich leise,
Ob noch nicht Vollendung sey? –
Ewigkeit schwingt über ihnen Kreise,
Bricht die Sense des Saturns entzwei.

3

The first stanza concentrates on the auditory aspects of the scene, the second on the visual. At the start, an unidentified speaker calls attention to a mysterious noise nearby. Suspense mounts as Schiller interposes two related similes comparing the strange sound to that of rushing water. Thanks to the peculiarities of German syntax, not until the last word of the first stanza does one discover that the mysterious sound is actually a human cry. At this moment, the tormented souls suddenly come into view. The speaker then describes the contorted expressions on the faces of a group of sufferers. Pain and despair lock their jaws in a perpetual curse. Their hollow eyes gaze fearfully, anxiously, toward the bridge over Cocytus, the legendary river of lamentation. Crossing this bridge represents their only hope for salvation.

The third stanza marks the poetic climax. Schiller finally makes explicit the fateful question that underlies both of the previous stanzas: will these torments ever cease? The devastating answer, written in the heavens above, is that punishment in Tartarus lasts forever.

The poem conveys an unusual kind of dramatic immediacy. From the speaker's opening "Listen!", the reader assumes the role of Virgil's Aeneas, witnessing the horrible torments of Tartarus directly. Yet the scene depicted is a static tableau. The suffering souls struggle to escape their misery, but time seems to have stopped, with the dramatic action frozen into a fixed image. Schiller's poetic depiction of "transfixed motion" captures the essence of their fate. Thus it is not a change in the circumstances of the damned souls that accounts for the dramatic quality of the poem, but rather the experience of the reader. The drama lies in the gradual discovery process that takes place from the first stanza to the last.

Schubert's musical setting intensifies the dramatic effect of the poem. The song is throughcomposed, with three distinct sections – differentiated through tempo, texture, meter, and rhythm – corresponding to the three poetic stanzas. Because the poetic stanzas do not have the same external structure, throughcomposition was a virtual necessity. But this untraditional song form has an interpretive function as well; each musical section portrays a different stage in the drama surrounding the fate of the damned souls in Tartarus. Suspense mounts until the denouement in the last stanza. Any large-scale musical repetition would contradict the rising tension and destroy the impression of an unfolding drama.

The extreme degree of chromaticism in the song, also foreign to traditional Lieder, helps to illustrate the agony of the damned souls. Schubert establishes this association immediately in the wildly turbulent piano introduction. The low groans that rise from the depths of hell are depicted with an ascending chromatic pattern that swells and recedes in regular intervals (Ex. 1). Although the song begins on open C octaves, any sense of a stabilizing tonal center is quickly lost. Indeed, it is difficult to tell whether the key signature indicates C major or – in the manner of recitative – no key at all. For most of the song, the vocal part doubles the slow, inexorable

Introduction

Ex. 1 Schubert, "Gruppe aus dem Tartarus" (D583), mm. 1–7

chromatic ascent of the accompanimental bass line. Rarely does it have any traditional sort of melodic character.

The Divine response in the last two lines of the poem coincides with a sudden shift to diatonicism. At the word "Ewigkeit," the tension-ridden dominant (to which the chromatic motion has ultimately ascended) finally resolves to a majestic C major tonic. Supporting the mighty octave leaps of the vocal part, the accompaniment sweeps up and down the keyboard in grand chordal arpeggios. Although the remainder of the song includes traces of the previous chromaticism, these passages do not threaten the harmonic stability. Diatonicism, associated with the deities in heaven, rules the day. The minor tonic chord with which the song concludes symbolizes

Ex. 2 Schubert, "Gruppe aus dem Tartarus" (D583), mm. 83–93

the essence of the harmonic battle fought and won (Ex. 2). The "chromatic" pitch E♭ enclosed within the stable tonic octaves at the final resolution no longer represents a disruptive force. Rather, it sounds the note of tragedy.

In almost every respect, "Gruppe aus dem Tartarus" forms a sharp contrast to the traditional Lied. The quasi-dramatic text, classical subject, throughcomposed form, intense chromaticism, unmelodic vocal line, and orchestral-sounding piano accompaniment suggest that this setting belongs to a different genre altogether.[13] The song may best be described as a "mixed-genre Lied," whose poetic and musical characteristics derive largely from dramatic compositional models. Possibly the *Allgemeine musikalische Zeitung* reviewer sensed this, for while he harshly criticized compositional eccentricities of the sort exemplified by "Gruppe aus dem Tartarus," the song nevertheless elicited his grudging admiration: "Op. 24, no. 1 text-paints in the beginning but does so quite well, and the modulations, although very harsh, are excusable, perhaps even justified, here."[14]

The reviewer had far less trouble comprehending Schubert's setting of Mayrhofer's "Schlaflied," Op. 24, no. 2 (D527).[15] This Lied, he asserts, comes "more or less near" to "actual song." In Schubert's day, "actual song" meant a simple, strophic Lied, such as those of the Berlin composers Reichardt and Zelter. Heinrich Christoph Koch's *Musikalisches Lexikon* of 1802 provides a concise description of the Lied's principal traits:[16]

> Lied. With this name one generally designates any lyrical poem of many strophes that is intended for song and associated with a melody repeated for each strophe, and that is capable of being performed by anyone who has healthy and not entirely inflexible vocal chords, without need of artistic instruction. It thus follows that a Lied melody should have neither so wide a range nor such vocal mannerisms and extended syllables as characterize the artificial and cultivated aria; rather it should express the sentiment in the text through simple but hence all the more efficient means.

As Koch's definition suggests, simplicity, popularity, and naturalness lie at the heart of the strophic Lied.[17] Intended to be sung by common folk rather than trained musicians, the Lied eschews musical artifice in favor of a plain, unpretentious manner. Koch's definition aptly describes many songs dating from the mid-eighteenth through early nineteenth centuries, including a substantial number by Schubert. One of these is Mayrhofer's "Schlaflied."

Typically, "Schlaflied" announces its genre affiliation in the title. The song is a lullaby, such as a mother might sing to her child (or, more accurately, an artistic recreation of a lullaby, since the song does not actually belong to the oral tradition). Here, uniqueness of expression is less important than appropriateness of gesture. Not surprisingly, the song shows similarities to other lullaby settings composed by Schubert and his contemporaries.[18]

Mayrhofer's poem conjures a peaceful pastoral scene in which a young boy falls asleep in a meadow:

Introduction

Schlaflied (translation on p. 139)

Es mahnt der Wald, es ruft der Strom:
"Du liebes Bübchen, zu uns komm!"
Der Knabe kommt, und staunt, und weilt,
Und ist von jedem Schmerz geheilt.

Aus Büschen flötet Wachtelschlag,
Mit irren Farben spielt der Tag;
Auf Blümchen rot, auf Blümchen blau
Erglänzt des Himmels feuchter Tau.

Ins frische Gras legt er sich hin,
Läßt über sich die Wolken ziehn,
An seine Mutter angeschmiegt,
Hat ihn der Traumgott eingewiegt.

Although the poetic speaker does not explicitly urge a drowsy child to fall asleep, as happens in most lullabies, the words nevertheless have this same intent. The tranquil imagery and repetitive verse structure create a soporific effect. And in the last stanza, Mayrhofer makes an implicit comparison between the boy asleep in the fields of Mother Earth and the child to whom the song is ostensibly sung, now presumably asleep in its mother's arms.

Schubert's use of strophic form (each poetic stanza set to the same musical strophe) is appropriate for several reasons. First, the poem comprises three stanzas with essentially the same external structure – borrowed from the tradition of folk poetry. Each stanza has four lines and the rhyme scheme aabb; each line is composed in iambic tetrameter with accented final syllables. In Schubert's day, it was generally expected that a poem comprising identically structured stanzas would receive a strophic musical setting.[19] Moreover, although the poem relates a short narrative, it sustains a single mood throughout. There is no need for a throughcomposed musical structure to depict contrasting poetic sections. The strophic repetitions, of course, also have an immediate functional purpose: to lull the listener to sleep.

Schubert's setting exemplifies several additional characteristics of traditional Lieder. The piano accompaniment, for example, has an extremely limited role. In this song, the melody appears solely in the vocal line. The piano accompaniment provides harmonic support and supplies rhythmic definition, but never doubles the tune. Nor does it engage in any clear text-painting.

Like most traditional Lieder, "Schlaflied" conveys an air of simplicity. For most of the song, the phrasing falls into regular four-measure groups.[20] The rhythmic patterns in both vocal part and piano accompaniment are simple and highly repetitive. The vocal declamation is primarily syllabic, never including more than two notes per syllable. With the exception of several quick modulations in the middle of the song, the harmonic progressions are routine, moving from tonic to dominant and subdominant and

8

back again. The brief journey through d minor, E♭ major, and f minor – a short chromatic interlude in an essentially diatonic setting – has no obvious textual stimulus. Schubert probably wanted to provide at least a small degree of contrast with the otherwise simple harmonies. On the whole, the song has the feel of a piece that anyone could sing.

Ex. 3 Schubert, "Schlaflied" (D527), mm. 1–2

In addition, "Schlaflied" exhibits features typical of lullabies. The meter (originally written as cut time, but later renotated as $\frac{12}{8}$ to clarify the sub-divisions of the beat) and slow tempo together create a rocking motion, suggestive of a baby's cradle (Ex. 3). For most of the song, this rocking motion is supported by the harmonic rhythm, which moves at a pace of two harmonies per measure. (During the chromatic modulations, there are four harmonies per measure, but these do not disrupt the overall effect.) The pianissimo dynamic, repetitive rhythmic patterns, and concluding tonic pedal point create a feeling of tranquility appropriate for a lullaby setting. The key of F major has, of course, long been associated with pastoral subjects.

"Gruppe aus dem Tartarus" and "Schlaflied" share almost nothing apart from their opus number and scoring for solo voice and piano. To call them both Lieder without differentiation is to say very little.

Most of Schubert's strophic Lieder were composed in 1815–16 and fall into the traditional subcategories of folk song, e.g., Wiegenlied, Liebeslied, Klaglied, Ständchen, Romanze, Trinklied, Barcarolle, Frühlingslied, Herbstlied, Winterlied, Morgenlied, Abendlied, Hochzeitlied, Arbeitlied, Schwertlied, Schwanengesang. Many of these songs have titles explicitly identifying the subcategory to which they belong, and all exhibit textual and musical characteristics traditionally associated with their type. They are generally simple and easy to sing. Some, in fact, have passed into the oral tradition.[21]

Schubert's interest in purely strophic settings began to fade in the late 1810s. During the 1820s, he composed an astonishing variety of modified strophic settings, which introduce certain changes into the musical repetitions, as well as many throughcomposed songs. Far fewer purely strophic settings date from these years.

As alluded to at the outset, Schubert's increasingly experimental approach to song composition perplexed his contemporaries. In the 1820s, the strophic Lied, with its strong link to German folk tradition, was still in various quarters regarded as the aesthetic ideal against which all songs should be measured. The mixture of genres was generally frowned upon. An article entitled "Über die Vermischung verschiedener Gattungen in der Musik," published by the Leipzig *Allgemeine musikalische Zeitung* in December 1807, states this position unequivocally: "The mixture of different genres is not simply an obstacle that one must avoid in the arts; it is rather a sin that the true talent never commits."[22] This attitude, typical of the generation,[23] accounts for much of the confusion and criticism that Schubert's dramatic songs frequently elicited. While some reviews of these songs were favorable, the introduction of dramatic elements within the framework of the Lied was not generally understood or perceived as a compositional advance. Indeed, when Zelter, known for his traditional strophic settings, died in 1832, critics sadly noted the passing of an age:[24]

> If, however, Zelter's Lieder have not been widely circulated, not properly valued, that is because very many no longer know nor take notice of what a true German Lied is and should be, because they have become accustomed to throw together all species of song. . .

While some writers focused solely on what had been lost, others were able to take the long view. Gottfried Wilhelm Fink, a long-standing critic of Schubert's stylistic eccentricities,[25] discussed the impact of Schubert's dramatic compositional style in a conciliatory review of the last two song cycles:[26]

> When one no longer feels satisfied with the continued existence of a thing, it is natural and true that all the boundaries are thrown into riotous confusion; as a result, much that is good dies, which the unbiased observer necessarily laments. It should be mentioned, however, that his lament is justified only so long as he does not lose hope of a new, more beautiful springtime and so long as he does not prejudicially and feebly reject the beneficial cleansing of the occasionally necessary storm. – So it is today with musical composition. Many of its otherwise blossoming regions have had their boundaries encroached upon. . . This fate has been suffered namely by the maternal, loving queen of song and particularly the gentle ruler of the fruitful realm of Lieder.

Like a purifying storm, the strong dramatic tendency of Schubert's Lieder had swept across all previous boundaries, revitalizing the domain of song.[27] Still enamored of the traditional Lied, Fink nevertheless glimpsed a "new, more beautiful springtime" in the wake of Schubert's efforts.

Fink was prescient. Schubert's fusion of elements from disparate vocal genres helped transform the Lied from folk song to art song – a genre which attracted nearly every major composer of the nineteenth century. By

incorporating dramatic poetic and musical traits into the traditional song setting for solo voice and piano accompaniment, Schubert raised the Lied from
its humble origins and broadened the horizons of musico-poetic expression.

Dramatic scenes, dramatic ballads, and mixed-genre Lieder

Schubert's experimentation with various kinds of dramatic song began
when he was a student at the Vienna Stadtkonvikt and continued until his
death. "Hagars Klage" (D5), the earliest surviving song for solo voice and
piano, depicts an episode from the Biblical story of Hagar and Ishmael.
Modeled directly after Johann Rudolf Zumsteeg's setting of the same text,
Schubert's song has an episodic musical structure built from alternating
passages of recitative and arioso.[28] These compositional styles lend the work
a theatrical quality foreign to traditional Lieder.

After "Hagars Klage," a host of dramatic songs followed. Many of these
works, such as "Szene aus Faust" (D126), "Antigone und Oedip" (D542),
and "Orest auf Tauris" (D548), fall into the category of dramatic monologues
or dialogues – both of which I shall call "dramatic scenes." Here, the words
of the song are ostensibly spoken by one or more identifiable dramatic personae who act out a particular episode. The song thus resembles an excerpted
segment of a larger musico-dramatic work.

A number of Schubert's early songs belong to a closely related vocal
genre, the "dramatic ballad". In songs such as "Der Taucher" (D77), "Der
Liedler" (D209), and "Ritter Toggenburg" (D397), the words and actions of
a set of characters are related by an anonymous narrator. The musical
settings, generally comprising alternating passages of recitative and arioso,
are in certain respects similar to those of dramatic scenes. However, the
single narrative perspective, manipulation of narrative time (e.g., through
flashbacks or foreshadowings), and use of "complete" poetic subjects in the
ballad give rise to a different set of compositional issues. Despite their musical
similarities, the scene and the ballad employ fundamentally different means
of representing story and action, and accordingly form distinct genres.

Schubert's interest in composing dramatic scenes and dramatic ballads
was strongest in the mid 1810s. While the ballad settings peaked in number
during 1815 (by far Schubert's most prolific year as a Lied composer), the
dramatic scenes continued to multiply through 1817, when his attraction
to Mayrhofer's classicist texts was most intense. Significantly, it was during
these years that Schubert's lifelong desire to become an opera composer
initially took hold. In 1815, after several juvenile attempts at dramatic stage
composition, he produced a string of short Singspiele: *Der vierjährige Posten*
(Körner), *Fernando* (Stadler), *Claudine von Villa Bella*, frag. (Goethe), and
Die Freunde von Salamanka (Mayrhofer). In 1816, Schubert worked on a
full-scale opera entitled *Die Bürgschaft*, based on the same subject as the
Schiller ballad setting from the previous year. Possibly Schubert viewed his

dramatic songs as a compositional prelude to writing operas, i.e., a small-scale musical arena in which to explore various techniques of dramatic composition. It seems no coincidence that shortly after his interest in composing dramatic scenes and dramatic ballads reached its peak, Schubert devoted much more of his time to opera. Two Singspiele (*Die Zwillingsbrüder, Die Verschworenen*), a melodrama (*Die Zauberharfe*), and three operas (*Sakuntala,* frag., *Alfonso und Estrella, Fierabras*) all date from the years 1820–23.

While Schubert's interest in composing dramatic scenes and dramatic ballads trailed off in the late 1810s, he had by no means exhausted his interest in dramatic songs. The lessons learned in writing these works appear to have fueled his imagination not only within opera but also in traditional Lieder. For beginning around 1814–15 and continuing throughout the 1820s, Schubert composed a large number of important songs that display a complex mixture of dramatic and lyrical traits. This loose group of works, which will be referred to generally as "mixed-genre Lieder," represents Schubert's most significant and original contribution to the history of song composition.[29]

While dramatic scenes and dramatic ballads can be defined with some precision, mixed-genre Lieder include songs exhibiting much greater variety. Works belonging to this more complex type of song, such as "Schäfers Klagelied" (D121) and "Der Doppelgänger" (D957/13), may initially seem to have little in common. In fact, they share a critical characteristic: the mixture of dramatic and lyrical (i.e., traditional Lied) traits. Although dramatic scenes and dramatic ballads also incorporate dramatic elements within a song setting, their primary link to the traditional Lied is the scoring for solo voice and piano accompaniment. Mixed-genre Lieder, on the other hand, display additional Lied traits: e.g., strophic repetitions, closed tonal structures, characteristic melodic or rhythmic patterns, subordinate accompaniment, periodic phrasing, and unity of mood. The inclusion of these traditional Lied traits has led to a more favorable reception of the mixed-genre Lieder than the straight dramatic scenes and dramatic ballads.

The boundary between dramatic songs (scenes, ballads, and mixed-genre Lieder) and other Lieder is sometimes difficult to discern. Recognition of genre is not an exact science; some songs fall into gray areas. Identifying a song's genre(s) is aided, however, by the fact that genres are never defined by just a single trait (musical or poetic). A Lied may have a through-composed or modified strophic form, like "Sprache der Liebe" (D410) and "Andenken" (D99), or depict an identifiable character, like "Aus 'Diego Manazares': Ilmerine" (D458), without being a dramatic scene, dramatic ballad, or mixed-genre Lied. (Many of these works are best described as cantatas, arias, or cavatinas.) A song's type emerges from a network of characteristics, involving both text and music.

Schubert's fusion of disparate musical traditions in his songs was naturally inspired by the individual poetic texts he chose to set. The depiction of identifiable characters, the inclusion of dialogue, the portrayal of action, the use of irregular verse forms – all of these factors demanded musical settings that went beyond simple *Sangbarkeit* and strophic form. The solution lay in borrowing compositional strategies from dramatic vocal genres.

Schubert did not aim to create a new genre, the dramatic song. If, in a particular Lied, he drew upon an array of compositional models – secco recitative, accompanied recitative, arioso, aria, folk song – he did so as a means of conveying to the listener his conception of the poem. Schubert may not have consciously recognized the various categories of dramatic song which form the subject of this study. This, however, in no way negates their usefulness as an interpretive tool.

Part I of this book focuses on dramatic scenes. Chapter 1 discusses the influence on Schubert of both neighboring genres and the dramatic scenes of his predecessors. Chapter 2 examines two contrasting examples of Schubert's dramatic scenes: "Szene aus Faust" (D126) and "Der Tod und das Mädchen" (D531). Chapter 3 describes the poetic and musical characteristics of Schubert's dramatic scenes, drawing examples from a variety of settings.

Part II offers a similar look at dramatic ballads. Chapter 4 surveys the history of the dramatic ballad before Schubert and discusses its influence upon him. Chapter 5 presents a close analysis of "Der Taucher" (D77). Chapter 6 describes the poetic and musical traits of the dramatic ballad.

Part III, devoted to mixed-genre Lieder, draws attention to some of the most important strategies Schubert used in his transformation of the genre. Chapter 7 focuses on lyrical songs with admixtures of dramatic traits and includes a detailed analysis of "Schäfers Klagelied" (D121). Chapter 8 concentrates on dramatic songs with admixtures of lyrical traits and contains an analysis of "Die junge Nonne" (D828). Chapter 9 discusses lyrico-dramatic songs, which embrace some of Schubert's greatest masterpieces. An analysis of "Pause" from *Die schöne Müllerin* (D795/12) shows Schubert to have created a whole new manner of expression, poised on the edge of dramatic declamation and lyrical song.

PART I

Dramatic scenes

Neighboring genres and dramatic scenes before Schubert

A bewildering array of genre labels have been applied to Schubert's song settings of dramatic monologue and dialogue texts. Writers use the terms dramatic scene, lyrical scene, Liedszene, scena, monody, solo cantata, and ballad, among others, to distinguish these songs from traditional types of Lieder. While some of these labels are misleading or inaccurate (as when "scena" is used for a song with a German text or "ballad" for a song with no single narrative perspective), they do draw attention to the close relationship between Schubert's dramatic monologue and dialogue settings and a host of neighboring genres. In groping for ways to describe these unusual Lieder, writers naturally borrow names of genres that employ many of the same dramatic compositional strategies.

The lack of uniformity in descriptions of Schubert's dramatic monologue and dialogue songs arises largely from the fact that the titles do not explicitly identify the genre. In this respect, these songs differ significantly from many traditional Lieder. Songs like "Frühlingslied" (D398), "Wiegenlied" (D498), "Schwanengesang" (D744), "Trinklied" (D888), and "Ständchen" (D889) announce their genre affiliation straight away. The title of "Iphigenia" (D573), on the other hand, while helping to signal genre, is inconclusive.

Schubert's dramatic monologue and dialogue songs are perhaps best called "dramatic scenes." This term has two advantages. First, the word "scene" appears relatively frequently in connection with these songs in the writings of both nineteenth- and twentieth-century critics. No other genre label appears as often. Secondly, the term helps convey the fundamentally *dramatic* aspect of the genre. In dramatic scenes, the words are ostensibly spoken by one or more usually identifiable personae who act out a particular episode. Action occurs. The song thus implies the dramatic progression of time, not its lyrical suspension. Songs by Schubert that fit this description are listed below.[1]

Songs which do not depict some kind of dramatic action are excluded from the genre. Thus "Julius an Theone" (D419), despite the operatic nature of its text and musical gestures, is best described not as a dramatic scene, but as an aria; no action takes place during the song. Nor may songs be identified as dramatic scenes simply because they are built from recitative

Dramatic scenes

Schubert's dramatic scenes

*more than one dramatic persona

D5	Hagars Klage (Schücking)	1811
D59	Verklärung (Pope, trans. Herder)	1813
D126	* Szene aus Faust (Goethe)	1814
D195	Amalia (Schiller)	1815
D282	*Cronnan (Ossian, trans. Harold)	1815
D293	*Shilrik und Vinvela (Ossian, trans. Harold)	1815
D312	*Hektors Abschied (Schiller)	1815
D322	*Hermann und Thusnelda (Klopstock)	1815
D323	Klage der Ceres	1815–16
D510	Didone abbandonata (Metastasio)	1816
D531	* Der Tod und das Mädchen (Claudius)	1817
D534	*Die Nacht (Ossian, trans. Harold)	1817
D540	Philoktet (Mayrhofer)	1817
D542	*Antigone und Oedip (Mayrhofer)	1817
D544	Ganymed (Goethe)	1817
D545	* Der Jüngling und der Tod (Spaun)	1817
D548	Orest auf Tauris (Mayrhofer)	1817
D564	Gretchens Bitte, frag. (Goethe)	1817
D573	Iphigenia (Mayrhofer)	1817
D674	Prometheus (Goethe)	1819
D699	Der entsühnte Orest (Mayrhofer)	1817?
D762	Schwestergruß (Bruchmann)	1822
D902/2	Il traditor deluso (Metastasio)	1827

and arioso, like "Trost, an Elisa" (D97) and "Die Sommernacht" (D289). These songs do not depict identifiable personae engaged in a particular course of action.

The influence of neighboring genres

Schubert's dramatic scenes perplexed his contemporaries because they differed so radically from traditional strophic Lieder. These songs become comprehensible once we recognize their generic origins. In setting dramatic monologue and dialogue texts, Schubert drew upon a number of different compositional models.

Several of his songs are patterned directly after the operatic scene, a dramatic genre that portrays a segment of action through the strict or free grouping of diverse musical elements, such as recitative, aria, duet, and chorus.[2] In the early nineteenth century, "operatic scene" had several meanings: (1) a highly dramatic passage of accompanied recitative leading to an expressive aria or ensemble, (2) both the introductory recitative and the succeeding number, or (3) a loosely constructed musico-dramatic episode, comprising a mixture of recitative, arioso, aria, duet, chorus, etc.

The first two meanings derived from the strict conventions of Baroque opera seria. In the early eighteenth century, operatic scenes generally depicted a single character engaged in a moment of high passion. The recitative established the dramatic context for the outpouring of emotion to follow. The conclusion of the aria marked the end of the scene, and the singer departed the stage after (it was hoped) a burst of applause.

The third meaning of "operatic scene" pointed ahead toward new developments in nineteenth-century opera. This more flexible conception, which had important antecedents in the dramatic works of Handel, Jommelli, Traetta, Gluck, and Mozart, allowed the music to follow the variable course of the dramatic action. Often involving both dialogue and chorus, the new type of operatic scene became especially common in the German Romantic operas of Weber, Spohr, Marschner, and Wagner.

Schubert wrote dramatic songs closely resembling both kinds of operatic scene. Not surprisingly, "Didone abbandonata" (D510), whose text comes from Act II, scene iv of Metastasio's similarly titled opera libretto of 1724, follows the eighteenth-century model. The song begins with a short, lyrical ritornello in the piano, followed by recitative. In these four lines of text, Dido chides Aeneas for his impending betrayal of their love. The recitative, interrupted by a recurrence of the ritornello and then a new impetuous accompanimental passage, opens in E♭ major but almost immediately forsakes this tonal center. After many harmonic twists and turns, the music finally arrives at f minor, the key of the following aria. During the aria, Dido grieves at the thought of her abandonment. Schubert's setting of these next eight poetic lines has an archaic feel. Composed in a quasi-ternary form, the aria includes much text-repetition and numerous opportunities for vocal display. The large vocal leaps and sustained high notes in Dido's powerful lament require the strength and range of a dramatic soprano.

"Szene aus Faust" (D126), a song setting of the Cathedral episode in Goethe's famous play, is reminiscent of the more freely structured nineteenth-century operatic scene. The text includes lines for Gretchen, an evil spirit, and a chorus, and the music embraces a corresponding diversity of styles. The structure of Schubert's setting does not conform to any conventional arrangement, as do the scenes in Baroque opera seria, but instead follows the unique course of action depicted in Goethe's text. (This song will be discussed in detail in Chapter 2.)

Songs resembling operatic scenes, particularly the eighteenth-century type, may have been more directly influenced by the concert scena. Like concert scenas, these songs are, or appear to be, extracted from a larger dramatic context.

During the 1770s and 1780s, the practice of performing operatic arias and scenes in the concert hall became widespread.[3] Audiences welcomed the custom because it allowed them to hear their favorite numbers over and over. These were typically the "Bravura" arias of the hero or heroine –

works that depicted a moment of high passion through the artifice of vocal virtuosity. It was, in fact, the virtuosic character of these pieces that made the practice feasible. For with the full dramatic context missing, the actual performer, rather than the character portrayed, attracted the listener's primary attention. Because of their musical extravagance, these works easily withstood the transfer from theatrical stage to concert hall.[4]

Not only were favorite operatic numbers extracted from recent stage works, but new dramatic vocal works were fashioned after the same compositional conventions. Like their operatic counterparts, these newly composed concert pieces quickly won general favour.

Inspired by Johann Christian Bach, Mozart composed many such works. Nearly twenty of them fit the description of what he himself called "scena": a virtuosic Italian concert aria of relatively large dimensions, introduced by accompanied recitative and sometimes an orchestral ritornello.[5] The texts are drawn from opera seria, especially the works of Metastasio, and depict climactic scenes charged with emotion and pathos. Similar works were produced by Haydn, Beethoven, Spohr, and Weber.

Schubert's setting "Il traditor deluso" (D902/2), one of three Italian songs for bass voice composed and published as a set in 1827, displays the same general structure as "Didone abbandonata." The song begins with an extended passage of accompanied recitative and concludes with a spirited aria in ternary form. The text is again by Metastasio, here taken from Part II of the sacred drama *Gioas re di Giuda*. In this case, however, Schubert's title obscures the identity of the speaker. Whereas with "Didone abbandonata" the listener was likely expected to recognize Dido and the dramatic context for her lament, "Il traditor deluso" involves no such assumptions. Like many concert scenas, the song can be appreciated on its own terms, without knowledge of the original dramatic source. "Il traditor deluso" is a wonderful virtuosic showpiece, and attention focuses as much on the actual singer as on the unnamed, outwitted traitor.[6] Significantly, the song was published with both Italian and German texts. This unusual tactic suggests an attempt to form a bridge between the Italian concert scena and the German Lied. As a dramatic scene, the song displays aspects of both.

A third compositional model for Schubert's dramatic scenes was the secular solo cantata, which had assumed a new dramatic manner in the late eighteenth century.[7] Before 1750, cantata texts were predominantly pastoral, humorous, or didactic. Composers regarded these kinds of subjects as most appropriate for domestic music-making or *Tafelmusik*, of which the secular solo cantata formed an integral part. But after mid-century, a new trend in cantata composition began to emerge. As the dramatic monologue based on mythological subjects eclipsed the prosaic cantata texts of previous decades, both German and Italian settings came to resemble large solo scenes for voice and orchestra.[8] No longer intended for amateur performance, the solo cantata now represented a demanding concert work for trained musicians.

Neighboring genres and dramatic scenes before Schubert

By the late eighteenth century, the traditional Neapolitan compositional model of two contrasting arias, introduced and separated by accompanied recitative, had given way to more flexible musical structures, freely arranged according to the dramatic dictates of the text. The large secular solo cantatas of Johann Gottlieb Naumann, Johann Christoph Friedrich Bach, and Johann Friedrich Reichardt, among others, comprise a fluid mixture of closed aria-like sections, extended arioso and accompagnato passages, and orchestral interludes. Frequent changes of key, tempo, texture, and meter, as well as colorful orchestration, permit moment-to-moment musical representation of the action and sentiments expressed in the poetry.

"Klage der Ceres" (D323), a song setting of an extremely lengthy Schiller text (comprising eleven twelve-line stanzas), might justifiably be called a solo cantata given its subject, style, structure, and scope. Like many secular solo cantatas of the late eighteenth century, the song is an extended monologue by a character from Greek mythology. Schubert's setting has a throughcomposed, episodic form, with contrasting music for the successive poetic stanzas. Passages of accompanied recitative alternate with lyrical sections and brief piano interludes. Only a few of the stanzas have closed tonal structures; most modulate away from the key in which they begin. Schubert makes no attempt to unify the piece tonally. The song begins in G major and, after numerous modulations, concludes in B♭ major. The many changes of key, tempo, meter, style, and accompanimental pattern help reflect the shifting moods of Ceres as she gradually comes to terms with her daughter's fate as queen of the Underworld.

Yet another dramatic vocal genre that left its mark on Schubert's Lieder was melodrama, in which words are *spoken* against or in the pauses of an orchestral accompaniment.[9] Initiated by Jean-Jacques Rousseau, the tradition of melodrama was further developed by composers such as Georg Benda and Johann Friedrich Reichardt, who wrote full-length melodramas in which the musical background creates an atmosphere of tension and excitement. In works such as Benda's *Ariadne auf Naxos*, the music also helps convey the wide range of emotions expressed in the text through harmonic audacities, extensive text-painting, and rudimentary leitmotifs. During the early nineteenth century, melodramatic passages began to appear in opera, where they heightened the dramatic tension in climactic scenes (e.g., the dungeon scene in Beethoven's *Fidelio* and the Wolf's Glen scene in Weber's *Der Freischütz*).

One of Schubert's songs, "Abschied von der Erde" (D829), was directly influenced by the tradition of melodrama. In this "song," an envoi to a one-act verse play by Adolf von Pratobevera, the words of the text are declaimed against the piano accompaniment. Schubert indicates in the score that each poetic line should coincide with one measure of music. The five four-line stanzas are separated from one another by brief piano interludes. The musical accompaniment itself is actually quite lyrical, forming a series of variations on a four-measure pattern made up of slow triplet rhythms. But

(lyrical)

by combining this accompaniment with spoken declamation, Schubert achieves a quasi-dramatic effect.

While the operatic scene, concert scena, secular solo cantata, and melodrama were all conceived for voice and orchestra, many individual works were published with the accompaniment transcribed for piano or harp. This practice is documented in early nineteenth-century music journals, as well as publishers' catalogues. In the first volume of the Leipzig *Allgemeine musikalische Zeitung*, for example, one finds a brief review of "Invocation à la nuit, scene de l'Opéra: Romeo et Julie, avec l'accomp. de Pianoforte, composée par Mr. Steibelt."[10] Several months later, the journal published a short description of "Le Départ, grande Scène, par G. Ferrari, avec Accompagnement de Piano ou Harpe."[11] With the orchestral accompaniment transcribed for piano, such dramatic vocal works obviously bear an even closer relation to Schubert's dramatic scenes.

Dramatic scenes before Schubert

In addition to neighboring genres, Schubert was certainly influenced by the dramatic scenes of other composers. Several of his dramatic scenes are in fact modeled directly after previous settings.[12] A brief survey of dramatic scene composition in the late eighteenth and early nineteenth centuries demonstrates that Schubert's monologue and dialogue settings, while unusual, were not novel.

Song settings of dramatic monologue and dialogue texts can be traced back to the mid eighteenth century. A salient example is the *Musikalischen Belustigung in dreißig scherzenden Liedern* (1758, 1765, 1767) of Valentin Herbing, cathedral organist at Magdeburg.[13] Straying from the strict compositional principles of the First Berlin School, this collection includes several dramatic duets and cantata-like solos that combine Lied and opera characteristics. The dramatic songs of Johann Philipp Sack, three of which appeared in Birnstiel's collection *Kleine Clavierstücke nebst einigen Oden* of 1760, were also composed during this period.[14] With their free mixture of accompanied recitative and measured lyrical passages, Sack's dramatic songs resemble the large monologues from contemporary opera.

The Viennese composers of the late eighteenth century occasionally wrote songs that may be described as dramatic scenes.[15] Mozart's "Als Luise die Briefe ihres ungetreuen Liebhabers verbrannte" (K.520), a fiery dramatic monologue for voice and piano, opens with a passionate operatic gesture entirely foreign to traditional Lieder. Sliding chromaticism, agitated rhythms, angular melodic lines, and an impetuous accompaniment supply an operatic aura to the forsaken lover's fury. Haydn's "Lines from the Battle of the Nile" (Hob.XXVIb:4), a recitative and aria for soprano or tenor and piano, is modeled directly after the concert scena. Beethoven's grandiose setting "Ah! perfido" (Op. 65), composed to a text adapted from

Metastasio's *Achille in Sciro*, was originally scored as a concert scena for soprano and orchestra but later recast as a song with piano accompaniment.

More important precedents for Schubert's dramatic scenes are found in the works of the Berlin composers Johann Friedrich Reichardt and Carl Friedrich Zelter, and the south German composer Johann Rudolf Zumsteeg. Although through most of his life Reichardt composed traditional strophic Lieder, in later years he wrote some throughcomposed settings of dramatic texts, including both individual poems and excerpted dramatic scenes.[16] Declamatory song settings showing the strong influence of Gluck first appeared in Reichardt's *Deutsche Gesänge* (1788). Others soon followed in the collection *Goethes lyrische Gedichte* (1794). Most significant were the "Deklamations-Stücke," as Reichardt himself called them, included in his last two song collections, *Goethes Lieder, Oden, Balladen und Romanzen* (4 vols., 1809–11)[17] and *Schillers lyrische Gedichte* (2 vols., 1810).

Declamatory songs in the third volume (headed "Vermischte Gesänge und Deklamationen") of the Goethe collection include the settings of "Prometheus," "Rhapsodie (Aus der Harzreise)," "Ganymed," "Gott (Aus dem Faust)," "An Lida," and "Alexis und Dora." The fourth volume (which bears no heading) contains two lengthy dramatic songs: "Monolog der Iphigenia" and "Monolog des Tasso." Similar works in the Schiller collection include two monologues of Thekla, two monologues of Johanna, "Aeneas zu Dido," and the dialogue "Hektors Abschied." All of these works, whether or not marked "deklamiert," have strongly declamatory vocal lines that mimic the irregular rhythmic patterns of actual speech.

The stimulus for the composition of these Deklamations-Stücke appears to have come from several sources. The freely structured verses of Goethe and Schiller obviously had a tremendous impact on Reichardt's compositional style. It is no coincidence that Reichardt's declamatory songs mostly appear in his last two Lied collections, based on the works of these poets. Goethe's *Stimmungslyrik* and Schiller's dramatic monologues impose demands upon musical settings very different from those of the pretty, sentimental verses of Hölty or Salis-Seewis.

Reichardt's Deklamations-Stücke were also probably influenced by the principles of melodrama. Not only did he compose full-scale melodramas (including Ramler's *Cephalus und Prokris* and Brandes's *Ino*), but he also occasionally introduced melodramatic elements within songs, as, for example, in Stolberg's "Thränen der Liebe." These works suggest that, even before his Goethe and Schiller settings, Reichardt was preoccupied with the question of how best to unite dramatic declamation and music.

Perhaps the most immediate inspiration for the Deklamations-Stücke was a performance of poetic recitations that Reichardt heard in Vienna during his visit there of 1808–09. In his *Vertraute Briefe*, Reichardt describes a "Musikalischdeclamatorische Akademie," presented on March 4, 1809, that radically altered his conception of the difference between speech and song.[18]

In addition to all these artistic goings-on, yesterday and the day before I happily attended several other public events. Madame Hendel and her companion, who calls himself Patrick Peale [Gustav Anton Freiherr von Seckendorff], gave the long awaited Deklamation in the small Redoutensaal, which was filled with an unusually brilliant audience. You know their kind of declamation. Herr Peale pleased me very much, especially with the narrative tone, in which he very finely held the delicate middle between painterly representation and dry narrative. Also I found more than I expected in his peculiar attempt to accompany the declamation with chords on the fortepiano and to incline and blend the modulations of the voice with those of the accompaniment. My ideas concerning the fundamentally different natures of speech and song were therewith shaken, and I was led to new contemplation. Yet it cannot be denied that in this new experiment the intentional effort to make the declamation approach song, without it actually becoming such, brought something monotonous and singsong-like to the declamation, which tended toward repulsive lamentation and whimpering, which in earlier times was so contrary to us in Ramler's exaggerated Deklamation.

By 1809, the performance of poetic recitations at musical concerts was no longer a novelty; poetic works had regularly appeared on concert programs for some time.[19] Accompanying these "declamations" with chords at the piano, however, was something new. Seckendorff's efforts to modulate his voice in accordance with the harmonic modulation of the keyboard accompaniment evidently had a striking effect, for the performance modified Reichardt's opinion of the aesthetic value of declamatory song. Significantly, Reichardt's own Deklamations-Stücke in the Goethe and Schiller collections appeared shortly after this performance.

Most of Reichardt's Deklamations-Stücke alternate declamatory and lyrical passages. His "Prometheus" setting serves as a good example. The song begins with an extended passage of secco recitative, marked "Kräftig deklamiert," during which Prometheus mocks Zeus's powerlessness (Ex. 4). Then, as Prometheus momentarily reflects upon his childhood faith in God ("Da ich ein Kind war"), the music adopts the lyrical character of arioso (Ex. 5). This change in musical style is inspired by the new contemplative tone of the text. Quickly, however, Reichardt reverts to the declamatory style. The rest of the song unfolds in accompanied recitative, with just one short measured passage near the end.

Reichardt's songs became well known in Vienna after his visit there in 1808–09. Schubert's acquaintance with these works is suggested by the inclusion of four Reichardt settings in Albert Stadler's important collection of Schubert's youthful Lieder.[20] Moreover, several of Schubert's dramatic songs, including both "Prometheus" and "Ganymed," show striking similarities to Reichardt's settings of the same texts.

Zelter's contribution to the tradition of dramatic song is considerably smaller.[21] Although much younger than Reichardt, Zelter had a more conservative musical taste. Throughout his career, he remained wedded to the Volkslied ideal of the First Berlin School. Zelter's four volumes of *Sämtliche*

Ex. 4 Reichardt, "Prometheus," mm. 1–4

Ex. 5 Reichardt, "Prometheus," mm. 22–25

Lieder, Balladen und Romanzen (1810–13) contain mostly simple strophic songs, plainly intended for the amateur performer.[22]

Several pieces, however, have a more dramatic, virtuosic character. "Margarethe," a setting of Goethe's "Gretchen am Spinnrade" monologue, is a large throughcomposed song with hints of strophic repetition. Schiller's "Die Theilung der Erde," a fable describing how the Poet earned a place in heaven, resembles a large solo cantata. Most significant is Zelter's setting "Kolma: Ein altschottisches Fragment aus der Liedern der Selma des Ossian," whose text was translated by Goethe into free German verse for inclusion in *Die Leiden des jungen Werther*. This long dramatic monologue depicts Kolma's lamentation in the wilderness upon discovering that her lover and brother have slain one another. Like a solo cantata, the piece progresses through a number of contrasting sections, organized in accordance with the dramatic action.

Zumsteeg, while best known for his ballads, also composed many dramatic monologues (or "monodies," as they are often called).[23] Three extended monologues, written during the 1790s, include settings of "Kolma" (Ossian/Macpherson, trans. Goethe), "Hagars Klage in der Wüste Bersaba" (Schücking), and "Iglous, der Mohrin Klagegesang" (Lafontaine). These monologues, published separately, closely resemble the dramatic ballads produced during the same period. They are large cantata-like works, built from alternating sections of recitative and arioso and featuring wandering harmonic schemes that mirror the course of the dramatic action.

In addition, various dramatic songs appeared in the seven volumes of Zumsteeg's *Kleine Balladen und Lieder* (1800–05).[24] Among these are settings of "Die Erwartung" (Schiller), "Maria Stuart" (from Schiller's *Maria Stuart*), "Ossian auf Slimora" (anon.), "Johanna" (from Schiller's *Die Jungfrau von Orleans*), "Anselmo" (from Gerstenberg's *Ugolino*), "Morgenfantasie" (Schiller), "Ossians Sonnengesang" (von Hoven), "Die Entzückung an Laura" (Schiller), "Lied eines Mohren" (Gerstenberg), and "Aus Meister Wilhelms Lehrjahren" (Goethe). While some of the texts derive from dramatic sources (the Schiller and Gerstenberg plays), others are individual poems written in a dramatic mode. As will be discussed in Chapter 4, Zumsteeg's dramatic songs – both scenes and ballads – made a particularly sharp impression on Schubert and served as a model for some of his own Lieder.

Song settings of dramatic monologue and dialogue texts drew mixed reactions from early nineteenth-century music critics. On the one hand, Reichardt's "Deklamationen" were generally well-received. An anonymous 1811 review of *Schillers lyrische Gedichte* called attention to his skillful handling of declamatory song:[25]

> Monologue of Thekla from *Piccolomini*, a large Declamation-piece, like the many for which we already thank Herr Reichardt, and where throughout one recognizes the masterly declaimer and cultivated, sensitive man, and also often the successfully bold and deeply touching artist. If one had to say which kind of form Herr Reichardt as a musician has uniquely perfected, it is this.

Other Reichardt "Deklamationen" singled out for praise in *Allgemeine musikalische Zeitung* reviews from 1809–11 include "Monolog der Iphigenia," "Monolog der Thekla" from *Wallensteins Tod*, "Erster Monolog der Johanna," "Prometheus," "Rhapsodie (Aus der Harzreise)," "Gott (Aus dem Faust)," and "Ganymed."[26]

Various writers, however, had misgivings about the value of extracting monologues from dramatic stage works and using them as song texts. Some monologues, they argued, were too intimately connected to their dramatic context and could not be understood when removed from it.[27] A song setting of a dramatic text would be justifiable only under certain conditions. One was if the dramatic subject were well known. An 1803 *Allgemeine musikalische Zeitung* review of I. P. Schmidt's setting of Johanna's monologue from Schiller's *Jungfrau von Orleans*, for example, explains that the success of the work depends upon the listener's presumed familiarity with the subject: "For what German, who has only some sense for poetry, has not become acquainted with Schiller's young maiden and particularly with this excellent monologue of hers?"[28] In addition, a composer might justifiably write a dramatic song setting if the meaning of the text were self-contained or if the words were of relatively little significance:[29]

> The Italians certainly do so often, particularly with scenes from Metastasio; and in hearing such single scenes, we feel less taken aback . . . [I]n part, many of the Metastasian monologues and large solo-scenes are already so separate and self-sufficient (good or bad) in the poem, that one can extract them without missing anything; in part, and most important, the composers treat the not seldom insignificant words so superficially, following only the general sense, and arrange the music so freely and independently (likewise good or bad) that, while listening, one pays little or no attention to the words.

If the monologue was too embedded in its original context, or the words were too important, critics claimed, a dramatic song setting was of dubious value.

In sum, Schubert's dramatic scenes were neither the first of their kind, nor the first to provoke criticism. While only a handful of these works were modeled directly after neighboring genres or song settings by other composers, all of them involve dramatic compositional techniques that challenged traditional conceptions of the Lied.

2

Two contrasting examples of Schubert's dramatic scenes

Schubert's dramatic scenes form a highly diverse group of works. The broad range of musical settings stems from the uniqueness of individual texts. Iphigenia's expression of sorrow at finding herself on the foreign shores of Tauris contrasts sharply with Prometheus' powerful mockery of the impotent gods in heaven, and consequently leads to a vastly different musical setting. But in spite of their differences, Schubert's dramatic scenes have much in common and can best be understood in conjunction with one another. The conceptual outlines of the genre emerge from consideration of two contrasting examples: "Szene aus Faust" (D126) and "Der Tod und das Mädchen" (D531).

"Szene aus Faust" (D126)

Goethe's "Szene aus Faust" (D126), which exists in two versions (both dating from December 1814), announces its genre affiliation in the title. Interestingly, this title did not originate with either the poet or the composer. Schubert's three autograph copies of the song each bear the heading "Aus Göthe's Faust." When the song was first published by Diabelli in 1832, four years after Schubert's death, the title was changed to "Szene aus Faust." This new title both clarifies and emphasizes the relation between D126 and Goethe's drama. Stressing this relation was appropriate, for Schubert's Faust setting has little in common with traditional Lieder.

The song encompasses all but the last line of scene xx from Part I of Goethe's *Faust*.[1] Schubert probably discovered the text while reading the play, for the text does not appear in any collection of Goethe's poems.[2] Thus when composing this Faust setting, Schubert presumably had the original dramatic context in mind.

The scene takes place in a cathedral, immediately following the death of Gretchen's brother. Wounded in a duel with Faust, Valentin dies bitterly reproaching Gretchen for her illicit relationship with Faust, which has ruined the family name. Gretchen, whose pregnancy makes her sin manifest, is mortified that her brother will not forgive her. She enters the cathedral seeking solace, but is immediately overwhelmed with guilt, externalized in

28

the form of an evil spirit. First taunting the poor girl with memories of her past innocence, the spirit then pricks her conscience with sly references to the mysterious circumstances surrounding her mother's death. (Gretchen had given the old woman what she thought was a sleeping potion – actually poison supplied by Faust – so that she could meet her lover at night.) With a choir in the background intermittently intoning verses from the Requiem Mass about the horrors of Judgment Day (an ironic commentary on the main focus of the drama, like that of a Greek chorus), the cathedral atmosphere becomes stifling. Gretchen grows increasingly hysterical and soon feels herself suffocating. At the end of the scene (omitted by Schubert), on the verge of fainting, Gretchen calls out for her neighbor's smelling salts.

Goethe heads the scene with a description of both its location and its participants: "Dom / Amt, Orgel und Gesang / Gretchen unter vielem Volk / Böser Geist hinter Gretchen." The text of the full scene runs as follows (translation on pp. 140–141):

> *Böser Geist.* Wie anders, Gretchen, war dir's,
> Als du noch voll Unschuld
> Hier zum Altar tratst,
> Aus dem vergriffnen Büchelchen
> Gebete lalltest,
> Halb Kinderspiele,
> Halb Gott im Herzen!
> Gretchen!
> Wo steht dein Kopf?
> In deinem Herzen
> Welche Missetat?
> Bet'st du für deiner Mutter Seele, die
> Durch dich zur langen, langen
>   Pein hinüberschlief?
> Auf deiner Schwelle wessen Blut? –
> Und unter deinem Herzen
> Regt sich's nicht quillend schon
> Und ängstet dich und sich
> Mit ahnungsvoller Gegenwart?
>
> *Gretchen.* Weh! Weh!
> Wär ich der Gedanken los,
> Die mir herüber und hinüber gehen
> Wider mich!
>
> *Chor.* Dies irae, dies illa
> Solvet saeclum in favilla. [*Orgelton.*]
>
> *Böser Geist.* Grimm faßt dich!
> Die Posaune tönt!
> Die Gräber beben!
> Und dein Herz,

Aus Aschenruh
Zu Flammenqualen
Wieder aufgeschaffen,
Bebt auf!

Gretchen. Wär ich hier weg!
Mir ist, als ob die Orgel mir
Den Atem versetzte,
Gesang mein Herz
Im Tiefsten löste.

Chor. Judex ergo cum sedebit,
Quidquid latet adparebit,
Nil inultum remanebit.

Gretchen. Mir wird so eng!
Die Mauerpfeiler
Befangen mich!
Das Gewölbe
Drängt mich! – Luft!

Böser Geist. Verbirg dich! Sünd und Schande
Bleibt nicht verborgen.
Luft? Licht?
Weh dir!

Chor. Quid sum miser tunc dicturus?
Quem patronum rogaturus,
Cum vix justus sit securus?

Böser Geist. Ihr Antlitz wenden
Verklärte von dir ab.
Die Hände dir zu reichen,
Schauerts den Reinen.
Weh!

Chor. Quid sum miser tunc dicturus?

Gretchen. Nachbarin! Euer Fläschen! –
[*Sie fällt in Ohnmacht.*]

A masterly portrayal of psychological tension, this climactic scene depicts Gretchen's confusion and remorse through the complex interrelationships of its various dramatic participants. At the beginning of the scene, Goethe describes Gretchen's position on stage as "unter vielem Volk." Standing amidst the devout congregation of worshipers, Gretchen feels the sting of her sinful isolation even more sharply than if she were alone. As a silent and forbidding presence – a ghostly reminder of her former self – the congregation intensifies the bitterness of her moral seclusion.

Gretchen's feeling of isolation from humanity deflects the drama onto a psychological plane. Although spoken, her lines represent an externalization of inner thoughts – a dramatic expedient known as soliloquy or interior monologue. Strangely, though, Gretchen's monologue is marked by frequent interruptions. Using a dramatic technique that dates back to medieval morality plays, Goethe turns the scene into a quasi-dialogue by embodying the pestering inner voice of Gretchen's conscience in an actual character – a vexatious evil spirit who whispers in her ear. Gretchen hears its nasty insinuations as a voice from within, but the audience sees it as an actual character.

The verses of the chorus (which, in direct contrast to the congregation, is heard but not seen) ostensibly bear no direct relation to Gretchen. Presumably she has entered the cathedral during a Requiem Mass, the occasion for which has nothing to do with her sorrowful predicament. Yet Gretchen hears the chorus's solemn chanting as a dire warning directed towards herself. Reverberating throughout the cathedral with support from the deep, somber tones of the organ, this ominous musical voice interrupts Gretchen's monologue in three different places, as if forcing its message upon her. Whereas only the evil spirit addresses Gretchen directly, the chorus serves as an equally effective dramatic vehicle for augmenting her sense of guilt.

In sum, the evil spirit represents a voice from within, the chorus a voice from without. As each competes for Gretchen's attention, the dramatic tension steadily mounts, leading eventually to her collapse.

Schubert seems to have wrestled with how to set this dramatic text. His first version, which survives in two manuscripts,[3] is an incomplete sketch rather than a finished work, as indicated by the phrase "Skizze zu einer weitern Ausführung" marked on one copy. Written mostly on two staves,[4] this version provides only a bare outline of the piano accompaniment. During the first eighteen measures, for example, the piano part consists of a simple bass line with full harmonies indicated in only four places. Even in those sections where the accompaniment attains a thicker texture, as in mm. 24–27 during Gretchen's first outburst, it remains confined to a single stave.

Scholars have argued that the manuscripts of the first version show that Schubert originally intended an orchestral setting for the song.[5] For one thing, both copies include various instrumental markings. In mm. 41 and 45, Schubert writes "Tromboni" next to the powerful, majestic chords in the accompaniment. Similarly, he adds the instrumental marking "Orgelton" to the purely accompanimental passages in mm. 35–39, 60–63, and 83–84.

In addition, the vocal writing suggests that Schubert conceived the piece for multiple singers: soprano, alto, and chorus. Although the parts for the evil spirit and Gretchen both appear in treble clef on the same staff, the vocal ranges differ considerably. The evil spirit, whose part dips down to b♭, sings primarily within the interval of a sixth above middle c'. Gretchen, who on one occasion reaches a high a", sings approximately an octave higher. Furthermore, the choral verses (which, like the other parts, are clearly labeled in the score) are set to four-part harmony, perhaps suggesting performance by a four-part choir.

Ultimately, however, these arguments remain inconclusive. There is no evidence that Schubert planned to write an opera on the Faust legend,[6] nor any direct evidence that he intended to compose a full concert setting with orchestral accompaniment. Significantly, the instrumental markings for trombone and organ which appear in the first version are taken directly from Goethe's text; no others are included. Only when the evil spirit exclaims "Die Posaune tönt!" does Schubert explicitly identify the sharp blasts of the "Tromboni". Goethe himself writes in "Orgelton" as a stage direction following the first entrance of the Chorus. Taking Goethe's hint, Schubert composes (and identifies) "organ" music after this and the next two choral entrances (Ex. 6). Perhaps, then, these instrumental markings should be regarded as a key to interpreting important passages in the piano accompaniment rather than notes for future orchestration.

Ex. 6 Schubert, "Szene aus Faust" (D126), 1st version, mm. 35–41

The fact that the evil spirit and Gretchen have different vocal ranges does not rule out performance by one singer. Schubert's setting of Goethe's "Erlkönig" (D328), composed just one year later, illustrates the flexibility of performance possibilities at that time. Although the ballad is usually sung as a solo, Schubert himself once participated in a quartet version.[7] The vocal ranges of the father and son contrast in much the same way as those of the evil spirit and Gretchen. Similarly, Schubert seems to have endorsed both solo and duet performances of Mayrhofer's "Antigone und Oedip" (D542), a song with two dramatic roles.[8]

The second version of the Faust setting is clearly intended for solo voice and piano.[9] That Schubert considered this version a finished work, requiring no further revision, is suggested by his having dated both beginning and end of the manuscript. Indeed, Schubert must have been satisfied with the work in its present form since he included it in the first book of Goethe songs sent to the revered poet in 1816.[10]

The second version makes a number of significant changes. Written on three rather than two staves, it clearly assigns all of the vocal parts to a single performer. The melodic range of the evil spirit is shifted slightly upward, facilitating performance of the work by one singer. Moreover, in the choral verses, Schubert does away with the possibility of a four-part choir by writing out a vocal line that doubles the top voice of the piano's chordal texture. (Of course, the work could still be performed with a unison choir.)

Interestingly, the piano accompaniment retains none of the first version's instrumental markings. The trombone and organ passages are themselves little changed; they are simply not identified in the score. The listener must discern the characteristic sounds of these two instruments in the "neutral" tones of the piano. No longer a bare sketch, the full-textured, richly motivic accompaniment now serves as an equal partner with the voice.

The second version of "Szene aus Faust" represents a dramatic scene in the guise of an art song.[11] Using the traditional Lied scoring of solo voice and piano, Schubert depicts a dramatic episode through imaginative suggestion. The singer assumes the role of an actor who plays not one but three parts: the evil spirit, Gretchen, and the chorus. The piano accompaniment, among its many functions, evokes the sounds of both trombone and organ. Schubert uses limited musical resources for multiple dramatic ends.

To prevent confusion, Schubert differentiates the three dramatic roles through musical means. Appropriately, the evil spirit and Gretchen, both of whom have speaking rather than singing parts in Goethe's play, deliver their lines in the declamatory manner of recitative. Neither character is ostensibly aware of the musical medium. The chorus, by contrast, chants its traditional Latin verses with measured pulse over a chordal accompaniment, reminiscent of an archaic church style.

The evil spirit's nasty insinuations are expressed in a variety of ways. The bitter irony of his opening lines (a teasing reminder of Gretchen's forsaken innocence) is conveyed through bare recitative (mm. 3–9). The simplicity of texture, as well as the C major tonality, evoke memories of the girl's untroubled past – days when she lisped her prayers with childish innocence.

But Gretchen's happiness is gone. The evil spirit's accusing tone, first hinted at through the rhythmic and melodic emphasis on "*Al*tar," "*Ge*bete," and "*Kin*derspiele," becomes explicit with the exaggerated stress on "*Gott.*" Suddenly the harmony falls prey to sinister chromaticism (mm. 10–11). Indeed, the evil spirit evokes Gretchen's happy memories only to drive the wedge of guilt more deeply into her consciousness. Gradually, his music slips into a fuller-textured accompanied recitative, marked by occasional text-painting. The descending chromatic bass line of mm. 15–20, for example, spells out death as the fate of Gretchen's mother, "die durch dich zur langen, langen Pein hinüberschlief" (Ex. 7).[12] Similarly, the quivering sextuplet pattern of the accompaniment in mm. 24, 26, and 28 represents the first movements of Gretchen's unborn baby, as well as perhaps her own shivering fear: "Und unter deinem Herzen / Regt sichs nicht quillend schon, / Und ängstet dich und sich / Mit ahnungsvoller Gegenwart?".

Ex. 7 Schubert, "Szene aus Faust" (D126), 2nd version, mm. 15–21

Gretchen's music, also accompanied recitative, illustrates her psychological instability. Her vocal line is characterized by rapid sixteenth note rhythms, dissonant harmonies, and rising chromatic motion, an apt musical portrayal of her growing hysteria (Ex. 8). Schubert also conveys the sense of suffocation she experiences in the cathedral. In mm. 51–54, as she pants, "Wär' ich hier weg! / Mir ist als ob die Orgel mir / Den Athem versetzte, /

Two contrasting examples of Schubert's dramatic scenes

Ex. 8 Schubert, "Szene aus Faust" (D126), 2nd version, mm. 29–32

Gesang mein Herz / Im Tiefsten löste," the accompaniment presents a string of dissonant harmonies, filling out two alternately diverging and converging chromatic lines.

The chorus – whose background chanting adds depth to the scene – has a distinct musical character as well. Intoning verses from the sequence of the Requiem Mass (verses 1, 6, and 7) to the ostensible accompaniment of an organ, it assumes the measured pulse, slow rhythms, and homophonic texture of an archaic church style (Ex. 9). Schubert does not actually base the chorus's music on traditional chant melodies. Indeed, he seems intent on preserving the anguished chromaticism of the other sections. Nevertheless, through continuous modulations, he captures a sense of free-floating tonality vaguely reminiscent of modal composition. (Especially suggestive are the "plagal" and "phrygian" cadences.)

The musical portrayal of multiple personae produces a striking dramatic effect. This effect is intensified by the illusion of a progressive time frame, arising largely from the instability of Schubert's music. The variable rhythms, irregular phrasing, shifting textures, and meandering modulations of the recitative passages have a strong forward impetus, mirroring the flow of the dramatic action. Even the choral music, with its homogeneous texture and paired phrases, wanders restlessly from one tonal center to the next.

Ex. 9 Schubert, "Szene aus Faust" (D126), 2nd version, mm. 33–40

Schubert also maintains momentum between different sections of the song. In some instances, a section ends with a dominant harmony that resolves at the entrance of a new character (mm. 32–33, 54–55). In other places, where a section concludes on a tonic chord, Schubert quickly undermines the harmonic stability by adding a seventh (mm. 44–45, 68–69).

The illusion of a progressive time frame is, of course, also built into the text. Of particular interest is the discontinuous chanting of the choir. For the four entrances of the choir, Goethe uses verses 1, 6, 7 (twice) of the sequence from the Requiem Mass.[13]

> 1 Dies irae, dies illa,
>> Solvet saeclum in favilla:
>> [Teste David cum Sibylla.]
>
> 6 Judex ergo cum sedebit,
>> Quidquid latet apparebit:
>> Nil inultum remanebit.
>
> 7 Quid sum miser tunc dicturus?
>> Quem patronum rogaturus,
>> Cum vix justus sit securus?

36

These verses were probably chosen for their special relevance to Gretchen's plight. Those verses of the sequence that do not help to magnify her terror and remorse are omitted. The particular choice of verses also serves another purpose: the leap from verse 1 to verse 6 suggests the passage of time. Presumably during the intervening speeches of the evil spirit and Gretchen ("Grimm faßt dich! . . ." and "Wär ich hier weg! . . .") the choir, off in the background, chants verses 2 through 5. Gretchen, one is led to suppose, simply does not hear them.

But is this scenario plausible? How can one account for the relatively short duration of the music between verses 1 and 6 of the choir? In Schubert's setting, the combined speeches of the evil spirit and Gretchen (mm. 45–54) take approximately the same amount of time as verse 1 (mm. 33–40). The presumed duration of verses 2–5 far exceeds the time allotted to the two speaking parts.

The apparent discrepancy between dramatic and musical time may be explained by the psychological nature of the scene. The interaction of Gretchen and the evil spirit represents the externalization of an inner dynamic: the self-torture inflicted by her conscience. The choir, on the other hand, represents a voice from the outer world which, at various intervals, forces its way into her consciousness. Like a dream sequence, the depiction of Gretchen's psychological turmoil moves at a different pace from that of "reality." What seems like a quick moment to Gretchen (mm. 45–54) corresponds to a much longer period in the real world of the chorus (the duration of verses 2–5).

The psychological character of this scene also helps explain Schubert's omission of the final line in Goethe's text: Gretchen's fainting cry, "Nachbarin! – Euer Fläschen!" Perhaps Schubert found this line too silly or trivial to serve as an appropriate ending for his song. There is, however, a more compelling explanation. The final line in Goethe's scene xx is the first line Gretchen utters that does not represent the externalization of inner thoughts. Here she actually speaks aloud to someone next to her. By ending the song just before this moment, Schubert keeps the drama on a psycho-logical plane. While ostensibly a segment of a larger musico-dramatic work, "Szene aus Faust" displays an aesthetic coherence of its own.

"Der Tod und das Mädchen" (D531)

Schubert's "Der Tod und das Mädchen" (D531), composed in February 1817, conveys a markedly different impression from "Szene aus Faust." Unlike D126, this song uses a text drawn from a non-dramatic source; Matthias Claudius's two-stanza poem originally appeared in the Göttingen *Almanach* of 1775. Because the setting consists of only forty-three measures and has a quasi-ternary structure and unified tonality, "Der Tod und das Mädchen" seems less of a departure from traditional Lieder. Nevertheless, it exemplifies many of the same characteristics as the Faust setting and is best described as a dramatic scene.[14]

Like many early nineteenth-century Lieder, "Der Tod und das Mädchen" depicts death as a welcome refuge from the turmoil of life. Showing the influence of Lessing and Herder,[15] the poem rejects the medieval conception of death as the harsh agent of punishment in favor of the more modern notion of death as a gentle and soothing sleep. To convey this message, Claudius casts the eight-line poem (translation on p. 141) in the form of a symbolic dialogue. The first stanza is spoken by a young maiden, representing life in its fullest bloom. The second stanza is spoken by the eerie skeleton figure of Death, representing the inevitable fate of human existence. While the maiden first reacts with alarm to seeing the bony image of Death lurking nearby, Death quietly reassures her that he has come to comfort, not to punish.[16]

> *Das Mädchen*
> Vorüber, ach, vorüber!
> Geh, wilder Knochenmann!
> Ich bin noch jung, geh, Lieber!
> Und rühre mich nicht an.
>
> *Der Tod*
> Gib deine Hand, du schön und zart Gebild!
> Bin Freund und komme nicht zu strafen.
> Sei gutes Muts! Ich bin nicht wild,
> Sollst sanft in meinen Armen schlafen!

The symbolic encounter of these two characters reveals death to be not an abduction, but rather an invitation to eternal rest.

While the poetic subject is typical of early Romantic Lieder, the dramatic mode of presentation is unusual. Lied texts are ordinarily presented from the perspective of a lyrical, anonymous "Ich." The words, emanating from a single consciousness, represent the outward expression of inner thoughts; the poetic speaker muses aloud, imparting a formal structure to the wanderings of his imagination. "Der Tod und das Mädchen," by contrast, involves two poetic speakers of sharply contrasting character. Far from the lyrical musings of an anonymous "Ich," the text constitutes a dialogue between interlocutors with distinct identities.[17] Like "Szene aus Faust," however, the song is composed for just one singer, requiring a leap of imagination on the part of the listener.

In setting this pseudo-dramatic text, Schubert naturally draws upon the stylistic vocabulary of operatic music. For the first stanza, when the maiden speaks, Schubert writes accompanied recitative, a dramatic style traditionally associated with moments of high passion. The maiden's panic at the sight of Death finds apt musical illustration in a series of short fragmented phrases (Ex. 10). Both the irregular phrase lengths and the syllabic declamation

Two contrasting examples of Schubert's dramatic scenes

Ex. 10 Schubert, "Der Tod und das Mädchen" (D531), 2nd version, mm. 8–21

help convey the breathlessness of her desperate appeal. The abrupt beginning, poignant appoggiaturas, pulsating chordal accompaniment, dynamic changes, and harmonic intensity of the first stanza are all characteristic of the accompagnato style.

Ex. 11 Schubert, "Der Tod und das Mädchen" (D531), 2nd version, mm. 22–25

Das erste Zeitmaß [Mäßig]

To portray the figure of Death in the second stanza, Schubert employs the distinctive pavane rhythm and recitational tone of the operatic oracle (Ex. 11).[18] Like the descending chromatic bass line, the pavane rhythmic pattern ♩ ♪ ♪ is one of Schubert's favorite musical symbols for death; he uses it numerous times throughout his songs in conjunction with references to death. The excessive repetition of this rhythmic pattern in "Der Tod und das Mädchen" both facilitates identification of the speaker and exemplifies Death's unyielding nature. Also illustrative of Death's character is the wholly un-melodic manner of the vocal line. This solemn recitation, contrasting sharply with the melodic arch of the vocal line in the first stanza, helps convey the other-worldliness of the speaker. The longer phrases, slower rhythms and tempo, lower range, pianissimo dynamic, and consistent texture of the second stanza all contribute to Schubert's musical portrait of Death.

Besides characterizing the two speakers, Schubert's setting also depicts their symbolic encounter. The music portrays the sequence of events marking the transition from life to death. The first hint of dramatic action occurs in the rounded eight-measure piano introduction, which essentially duplicates the musical material of the second stanza. Although, on a first hearing, one does not yet recognize this as Death's music, the familiar pavane rhythm, slow tempo, and minor mode create a foreboding atmosphere. When the maiden cries out, "Vorüber, ach, vorüber! / Geh, wilder Knochenmann!", it becomes clear that Death has already arrived on the scene. Schubert thus makes explicit what is implicit in the text – that something happens before the beginning of the first stanza: Death sneaks up on the young girl.

The rhythmic transformation of mm. 16–19 illustrates how the maiden succumbs to Death. During the last line of the maiden's stanza, Schubert

Two contrasting examples of Schubert's dramatic scenes

Ex. 12 Schubert, "Der Tod und das Mädchen" (D531), 2nd version, mm. 34–43

replaces the pulsing eighth note rhythms of the piano accompaniment with the pavane pattern associated with Death. This change in accompanimental rhythm, combined with the shift in poetic tone suggested by "geh, Lieber!", indicates that the girl's resistance has melted. The actual touch of death seems to coincide with her phrase "rühre mich nicht an," for it is exactly here that the pavane rhythm reappears. After the textual repeat in mm. 18–19, the maiden becomes silent: her voice is echoed in the accompaniment for two measures before Death begins to speak.

To illustrate the actual benevolence of Death, Schubert directs the opening d minor harmony of the second stanza through several major sonorities – first F, then B♭, and finally D major. In the major mode, Death's music takes on the character of a lullaby, with the ponderous pavane rhythms now suggesting the gentle rocking motion of a slumber song (Ex. 12). The maiden, we are led to imagine, lies eternally asleep in Death's protective arms.

The preceding analyses of "Szene aus Faust" and "Der Tod und das Mädchen" illustrate various ways music and text interact to depict character and action in Schubert's dramatic scenes. They also demonstrate the wide range of settings embraced by this vocal genre. "Szene aus Faust," with its abrupt opening, recitative, meandering tonal scheme, and throughcomposed form, resembles a scene from an early German Romantic opera. Because of its brevity, quasi-ternary form, and unified tonality, "Der Tod und das Mädchen" has a very different feel. It too, however, employs dramatic compositional styles (accompanied recitative and the recitational tone of the operatic oracle) with great success. The two settings share an array of poetic and musical traits – traits which help to identify dramatic scenes in general.

3

Poetic and musical traits of the dramatic scene

The assortment of poetic and musical traits that typify the dramatic scene may be grouped into five principal characteristics: (1) setting of a dramatic text for solo voice and piano, (2) depiction of dramatic personae, (3) portrayal of action, (4) description of mise-en-scène, and (5) representation of a dramatic segment.[1] No single *musical* trait belongs exclusively to the dramatic scene. Many musical characteristics of these songs are also found, for example, in the dramatic ballad. But there are certain poetic traits that distinguish the dramatic scene from related song types. By exploring the genre's principal characteristics, we arrive at a clearer understanding of its unique conception.

Dramatic text

The texts for Schubert's dramatic scenes derive from works intended for stage performance as well as from other sources.[2] Dramatic monologues excerpted from plays and opera libretti include the texts of "Amalia" (D195) (Schiller, *Die Räuber*, III, i), "Gretchens Bitte" (D564) (Goethe, *Faust*, Pt. I, xviii), "Didone abbandonata" (D510) (Metastasio, *Didone abbandonata*, II, iv), and "Il traditor deluso" (D902/2) (Metastasio, *Gioas re di Giuda*, Pt. II).[3] "Szene aus Faust" (D126), as we have noted, constitutes an entire scene in Goethe's drama (*Faust*, Pt. I, xx). Several songs bear an indirect relationship to dramatic stageworks. An early version of the dialogue text of "Hektors Abschied" (D312) appears in Act II, scene ii of Schiller's *Die Räuber*.[4] Goethe's dramatic monologue "Prometheus" (D674) maintains an ambiguous link to an unfinished Prometheus drama, begun in 1773.[5]

Of course, not all songs with texts originally intended for stage performance constitute dramatic scenes. Many such works are best described as arias (e.g., "Son fra l'onde" [D78]), ballads ("Der König in Thule" [D367] and "Erlkönig" [D328]), love songs ("Die Liebe" [D210]), hunting songs ("Jagdlied" [D521]), serenades ("Ständchen" [D889]), drinking songs ("Trinklied" [D888]), Singspiellieder ("Wer kauft Liebesgötter" [D261]), or nocturnes ("Bertas Lied in der Nacht" [D653]). It is the dramatic *quality* of a particular text, not the mere fact that the text derives from a play or opera libretto, that signals the dramatic scene.

Many of Schubert's song texts drawn from sources not intended for stage performance have precisely this quality. These sources include prose-poems (e.g., "Shilrik und Vinvela" [D293]), essays ("Verklärung" [D59]), almanacs ("Der Tod und das Mädchen" [D531]; "Hagars Klage" [D5]), and manuscripts (all of the Mayrhofer settings).[6] While the texts themselves exhibit diverse characteristics and may be classified under a variety of genre headings e.g., Kantate, Ode, grosse Hymne, Wechselgesang, Gespräch, Monolog, Rollenlied, Stimmungslied), they share an important trait: a dramatic mode of presentation.[7]

Many definitions of "dramatic" have been advanced, stressing variously the temporal aspect, the representation of action, the relation between poet and persona, and the role of the audience, among other things.[8] For our purposes, the brief definition given in Aristotle's *Poetics* is most illuminating. According to Aristotle, the various arts "differ from one another in three respects – the medium, the objects, the manner or mode of imitation."[9] The last category distinguishes dramatic poetry. "For the medium being the same, and the objects the same, the poet may imitate by narration . . . or he may present all his characters as living and moving before us."[10] This notion of the dramatic applies to Schubert's dramatic scenes. Whatever the textual source, the songs create an illusion of actual characters "living and moving before us," who speak their thoughts directly, rather than through the voice of a narrator.

One example is "Hagars Klage" (D5), Schubert's earliest surviving song. Schücking's nineteen-stanza poem concerns the story of Hagar and Ishmael, related in Genesis 21. Hagar delivers this lengthy monologue from the wasteland to which she and her son have been banished. The first four stanzas run as follows:

> Hier am Hügel heißen Sandes,
> Sitz' ich, und mir gegenüber
> Liegt mein sterbend Kind!
>
> Lechzt nach einem Tropfen Wasser,
> Lechzt und ringt schon mit dem Tode,
> Weint, und blickt mit stieren Augen
> Mich bedrängte Mutter an!
>
> Du mußt sterben, armes Würmchen,
> Ach, nicht eine Thräne
> Hab' ich in den trocknen Augen,
> Wo ich dich mit stillen kann!
>
> Ha! säh' ich eine Löwenmutter
> Ich wollte mit ihr kämpfen,
> Kämpfen mit ihr um die Eiter.

Hagar speaks in her own voice rather than acting as the mouthpiece of the poet. Her character is so individualized that one can easily imagine the monologue delivered on stage. Direct speech by identifiable personae, as occurs in "Hagars Klage," represents a fundamental trait of nearly all of Schubert's dramatic scenes.

Unlike the mode of presentation, the structural aspects of dramatic scene texts vary greatly from work to work. The texts may or may not be constructed in stanzas, and may or may not have a regular meter or rhyme scheme.[11] One song with a highly regular textual structure is "Hektors Abschied" (D312), a dialogue between the classical figures of Andromache and Hector before the latter's departure for war. The text comprises four six-line stanzas, alternating between the two characters. Written in trochaic pentameter, each stanza has the same rhyme scheme and pattern of stresses at line endings.[12]

> *Andromache*
> Will sich Hektor ewig von mir wenden,
> Wo Achill mit den unnahbar'n Händen
> Dem Patroklus schrecklich Opfer bringt?
> Wer wird künftig deinen Kleinen lehren
> Speere werfen und die Götter ehren,
> Wenn der finstre Orkus dich verschlingt?
>
> *Hektor*
> Theures Weib, gebiete deinen Thränen!
> Nach der Feldschlacht ist mein feurig Sehnen,
> Diese Arme schützen Pergamus.
> Kämpfend für den heil'gen Herd der Götter
> Fall ich, und des Vaterlandes Retter
> Steig' ich nieder zu dem styg'schen Fluß.
>
> *Andromache*
> Nimmer lausch' ich deiner Waffen Schalle,
> Müßig liegt dein Eisen in der Halle,
> Priams großer Heldenstamm verdirbt.
> Du wirst hingeh'n, wo kein Tag mehr scheinet,
> Der Cocytus durch die Wüsten weinet,
> Deine Liebe im Lethe stirbt.
>
> *Hektor*
> All mein Sehnen will ich, all mein Denken,
> In des Lethe stillen Strom versenken,
> Aber meine Liebe nicht.
> Horch! der Wilde tobt schon an den Mauern,
> Gürte mir das Schwerdt um, laß das Trauern!
> Hektors Liebe stirbt im Lethe nicht.

Goethe's "Prometheus" (D674), written in free verse, stands in sharp contrast to Schiller's classical dialogue. Prometheus' monologue has neither stanzas nor a regular rhyme scheme. The individual lines, composed in a loose iambic meter, vary in length.

Bedecke deinen Himmel, Zeus,
Mit Wolkendunst,
Und übe, dem Knaben gleich,
Der Disteln köpft,
An Eichen dich und Bergeshöhn;
Mußt mir meine Erde
Doch lassen stehn,
Und meine Hütte, die du nicht gebaut,
Und meinen Herd,
Um dessen Gluth
Du mich beneidest.

Ich kenne nichts Ärmeres
Unter der Sonn' als euch, Götter!
Ihr nähret kümmerlich
Von Opfersteuern
Und Gebetshauch
Eure Majestät,
Und darbtet, wären
Nicht Kinder und Bettler
Hoffnungsvolle Thoren.

Da ich ein Kind war,
Nicht wußte wo aus noch ein,
Kehrt' ich mein verirrtes Auge
Zur Sonne, als wenn drüber wär'
Ein Ohr, zu hören meine Klage,
Ein Herz, wie mein's,
Sich des Bedrängten zu erbarmen.

Wer half mir
Wider der Titanen Übermuth?
Wer rettete vom Tode mich,
Von Sklaverey?
Hast du nicht Alles selbst vollendet,
Heilig glühend Herz?
Und glühtest jung und gut,
Betrogen, Rettungsdank
Dem Schlafenden da droben?

Ich dich ehren? Wofür?
Hast du die Schmerzen gelindert
Je des Beladenen?
Hast du die Thränen gestillet
Je des Geängsteten?
Hat mich nicht zum Manne geschmiedet
Die allmächtige Zeit
Und das ewige Schicksal,
Meine Herrn und deine?

Wähntest du etwa,
Ich sollte das Leben hassen,
In Wüsten fliehen,
Weil nicht alle
Blütenträume reiften?

Hier sitz' ich, forme Menschen
Nach meinem Bilde,
Ein Geschlecht, das mir gleich sey,
Zu leiden, zu weinen,
Zu genießen und zu freuen sich,
Und dein nicht zu achten,
Wie ich!

The loose structure of the poem corresponds to its subject. Prometheus' fierce denial of the gods' power and his assertion of autonomy are naturally at odds with any external strictures on the mode of expression. The free verse in which Prometheus speaks serves as a linguistic embodiment of the creative freedom toward which he strives.

The Ossian dialogue "Shilrik und Vinvela" (D293) is actually composed in prose, with no regular metrical pattern at all.[13] In the opening two segments of the text, Vinvela approaches her warrior-lover:

Vinvela
Mein Geliebter ist ein Sohn des Hügels; er verfolgt die fliehenden Hirsche; die Doggen schnauben um ihn; die Senn seines Bogens schwirrt in dem Wind. Ruhst du bei der Quelle des Felsen, oder beim Rauschen des Bergstroms? Der Schilf neigt sich im Wind, der Nebel fliegt über die Heide; ich will ihm ungesehn nahn; ich will ihn betrachten vom Felsen herab. Ich sah dich zuerst liebreich bei der veralteten Eiche von Branno; schlank kehrtest du vom Jagen zurück, unter allen deinen Freunden der schönste.

Shilrik
Was ist's für eine Stimme, die ich höre? Sie gleicht dem Hauche des Sommers! Ich sitz nicht beim neigenden Schilfe; ich hör nicht die Quelle des Felsen. Ferne, ferne Vinvela, geh ich zu den Kriegen von Fingal: meine Doggen beleiten mich nicht; ich trete nicht mehr auf den Hügel. Ich seh dich nicht mehr von der Höhe, zierlich schreitend am Strome der Fläche; schimmernd, wie der Bogen des Himmels; wie der Mond auf der westlichen Welle.

The vast structural differences among these three poetic texts do not preclude the possibility of the songs belonging to the same genre. As we shall see, Schubert's dramatic scenes are in large measure characterized by the very looseness of their forms. The musical settings often subvert rather than support the structural outlines of the texts. As a rule, the tempo and shape of the dramatic action are far more important than the formal features of the text.

Whereas the structural aspects of dramatic scene texts differ from work to work, the subjects are far less varied. The majority of Schubert's dramatic scenes involve subjects drawn from classical mythology. In this respect, the genre resembles eighteenth-century opera seria, including Gluck's reform opera which Schubert greatly admired. A smaller number of songs derive their subjects from Scottish and Germanic legendry, which was in vogue during Schubert's day.

Principal subjects of Schubert's dramatic scenes

(a) *Classical mythology*

D312	Hektors Abschied (Schiller)
D323	Klage der Ceres (Schiller)
D510	Didone abbandonata (Metastasio)
D540	Philoktet (Mayrhofer)
D542	Antigone und Oedip (Mayrhofer)
D544	Ganymed (Goethe)
D548	Orest auf Tauris (Mayrhofer)
D573	Iphigenia (Mayrhofer)
D674	Prometheus (Goethe)
D699	Der entsühnte Orest (Mayrhofer)

(b) *Scottish and Germanic legend*

D126	Szene aus Faust (Goethe)
D282	Cronnan (Ossian)
D293	Shilrik und Vinvela (Ossian)
D322	Hermann und Thusnelda (Klopstock)
D534	Die Nacht (Ossian)
D564	Gretchens Bitte (Goethe)

Because dramatic scenes portray only a short segment of action, the subject must be well known. The listener is expected to recognize the episode and to imagine the full dramatic context. It is no coincidence that Schubert's dramatic scenes depict subjects drawn from myths and legends, and, to a lesser extent, from contemporary drama and traditional allegory. Contemporary audiences had little difficulty recognizing the plight of characters such as Iphigenia, Gretchen, or Prometheus.

Dramatic personae

The representation of dramatic personae is a nearly universal characteristic of Schubert's dramatic scenes. Rather than posing as an anonymous "I," the poetic speaker assumes a unique identity, critical to the action of the song.

Sometimes the dramatic situation alone identifies the poetic speaker. A speaker who contemptuously flaunts his own creative power in the face of an impotent Zeus is surely Prometheus. A speaker who finds himself on the island of Tauris, pursued by the Furies, implicitly identifies himself as Orestes. Occasionally the dramatic personae are actually named in the text, e.g., "Hektors Abschied" (D312) ("Will sich Hektor ewig von mir wenden") and "Szene aus Faust" (D126) ("Wie anders, Gretchen, war dirs"). In any event, Schubert generally uses song titles (mostly the same as the original poetic titles) that identify the characters straight away: e.g., "Hagars Klage" (D5), "Hermann und Thusnelda" (D322), "Klage der Ceres" (D323), "Antigone und Oedip" (D542), "Ganymed" (D544), "Iphigenia" (D573),

"Prometheus" (D674). In a few cases, such as "Der Tod und das Mädchen" (D531) and "Schwestergruß" (D762), the title alludes instead to a character type. Although here the speakers' identities remain partially obscure, the titles nevertheless focus attention on specific dramatic personae.

Significantly, only a handful of Schubert's dramatic scenes have anything resembling a genre title: "*Szene* aus Faust" (D126), "Hagars *Klage*" (D5), "*Klage* der Ceres" (D323), "Gretchens *Bitte*" (D564). Genre titles stress the relationship between the work in question and other similar works; they focus the listener's attention on shared compositional conventions. Schubert's dramatic scenes, however, are rigorously individualistic. They depict specific characters in unique situations. Hence, genre titles are for the most part avoided.[14] Interestingly, even those few titles that do mention genre couple that heading with the character's name.

The number of personae depicted in a dramatic scene is flexible. Some works portray a single character, others several. Initially, these may seem to represent very different types of song. Dramatic monologues, which involve a one-to-one correspondence between character and performer, are analogous to operatic arias presented in concert version. The singer substitutes directly for the actor on stage. In dramatic dialogues, one singer substitutes for two or more actors by alternating among several roles.

In light of these different performing (and listening) tasks, it is tempting to distinguish between monologue settings, like " Prometheus" (D674), and dialogue settings, like "Hermann und Thusnelda" (D322). This genre distinction proves unfounded. Some dialogue songs, such as "Hektors Abschied" (D312) and "Antigone und Oedip" (D542), were apparently performed in Schubert's day as both solos and duets. Moreover, many dialogue songs display a closer relationship to monologue songs than to each other. "Szene aus Faust" (D126), for example, has as much if not more in common with Schubert's other Faust songs – "Gretchen am Spinnrade" (D118) and "Gretchens Bitte" (D564) – as with "Der Tod und das Mädchen" (D531). Thus it makes little sense to separate monologue and dialogue songs. The genre encompasses them both.[15]

The personae in dramatic scenes, unlike those in traditional song types, such as the lullaby, serenade, or hymn, are ostensibly unaware of the musical medium through which they express themselves. Like most operatic characters, they imagine that they are speaking, not singing. Consequently, the vocal lines are often declamatory, mimicking the effect of actual speech.

In many settings, Schubert uses recitative for the representation of action and for emphatic statements, and arioso for the expression of lyrical sentiments. "Verklärung" (D59), which depicts a human soul ascending to heaven at the moment of death, demonstrates the characteristic alternation of contrasting musical styles. The poem contains three stanzas, the first with eight lines and both the second and third with six lines. This structure is obscured, however, by the stylistic changes in the musical setting:

recit.	Lebensfunke, vom Himmel entglüht,
	Der sich loszuwinden müht!
	Zitternd, kühn, vor Sehnen leidend,
	Gern und doch mit Schmerzen scheidend –
	End' o end' den Kampf, Natur!
arioso	Sanft ins Leben
	Aufwärts schweben,
	Sanft hinschwinden laß mich nur.
recit.	Horch! mir lispeln Geister zu:
arioso	"Schwester-Seele! komm zur Ruh!"
recit.	Ziehet was mich sanft von hinnen?
	Was ists, das mir meine Sinnen,
	Mir den Hauch zu rauben droht?
	Seele sprich, ist das der Tod?
	Die Welt entweicht! Sie ist nicht mehr!
arioso	Engel-Einklang um mich her!
	Ich schweb' im Morgenroth –
	Leiht, o leiht mir eure Schwingen,
	Ihr Brüder-Geister! helft mir singen:
recit.	"O Grab, wo ist dein Sieg? wo ist dein Pfeil, o Tod?"

Those parts of the text which express gentle emotions (lines 6–8, 10, 16–19) are set in the metrically regular, lyrical manner of arioso. The dramatic opening statement, the actual moment of transition from life to death, and the emphatic final line are set in secco recitative. The operatic associations of these two vocal styles help sustain the illusion that the monologue is spoken rather than sung.

Finally, the personae in dramatic scenes express themselves in a manner emphasizing their individuality. Schubert conveys Prometheus' fiercely rebellious nature through the highly irregular rhythms and chromaticism of his vocal line (Ex. 13a and 13b). The powerful dissonant sonorities, unusual harmonic progressions, and thundering tremolos in the keyboard accompaniment contribute to the musical portraiture. Iphigenia, by contrast, expresses her thoughts with a sweet nobility of tone. Her vocal line is slightly melismatic and follows a more conventional melodic shape (Ex. 14). Large vocal leaps and frequent appoggiaturas intensify the poignancy of her plight. Oedipus, the once heroic king, recalls his former days of glory with triumphant triplet rhythms, bold C major harmonies, and hunting call motives in the keyboard accompaniment (Ex. 15). In each song, the musical setting compensates for the lack of costumes and physical props by creating a detailed (if sometimes conventional) sound-picture of the characters represented.

Ex. 13a Schubert, "Prometheus" (D674), mm. 6

Be - dec - ke dei - nen Him - mel, Zeus,___ mit Wol - ken dunst,

Ex. 13b Schubert, "Prometheus" (D674), mm. 78–82

Hat mich nicht zum Man - ne ge - schmie - det die all - mäch - ti - ge

Zeit und das e - wi - ge Schick - sal, mei - ne Herrn und dei - ne?

Dramatic Action

Representation of action is also a central trait of the dramatic scene. Unlike the traditional operatic aria or strophic Lied, which typically have static subjects, the dramatic scene portrays an episode in which things change. Whereas the aria and strophic Lied create an illusion of "suspended time," as if all action had temporarily come to a halt, the dramatic scene suggests the opposite. Time advances and, during the course of the song, the dramatic

51

Ex. 14 Schubert, "Iphigenia" (D573), mm. 1–6

situation progresses to a new stage. In sum, the text creates an illusion of actual drama – of characters presently engaged in particular actions.

To support the illusion of dramatic action, Schubert usually sets each stanza or section of the text set to new music. Because it enables the moment-to-moment representation of textual details, throughcomposition is especially conducive to dramatic subjects. Each new phase of the action finds unique musical expression. For those songs without stanzaic texts, throughcomposed

Poetic and musical traits of the dramatic scene

Ex. 15 Schubert, "Antigone und Oedip" (D542), mm. 52–59

Trank ich in schö - nen Ta - gen nicht in mei - ner

gro - ßen Vä - ter Hal - le, beim Hel - den

form is a virtual necessity – free verse and prose do not lend themselves to strophic or even modified strophic settings. But even those dramatic scenes with stanzaic texts are generally throughcomposed. The musical form is induced by the dramatic nature of the subject.

A comparison of two songs, one throughcomposed and the other not, helps illustrate the dramatic effect of throughcomposition. "Antigone und Oedip" (D542) comprises two separate monologues. The first is spoken by Antigone, who pleads with the gods to pity her blind, suffering father, Oedipus, and to vent their anger on herself instead. The second is spoken by Oedipus, who, upon waking from a troubled sleep, foresees his doom at Colonos.

Dramatic scenes

Antigone
Ihr hohen Himmlischen erhöret
Der Tochter herzentströmtes Flehen;
Laßt einen kühlen Hauch des Trostes
In des Vaters große Seele wehn.

Genüget, euren Zorn zu sühnen,
Dies junge Leben – nehmt es hin;
Und euer Rachestrahl vernichte
Die tiefbetrübte Dulderin.

Demütig falte ich die Hände –
Das Firmament bleibt glatt und rein,
Und stille ist's, nur laue Lüfte
Durchschauern noch den alten Hain.

Was seufzt und stöhnt der bleiche Vater?
Ich ahn's – ein furchtbares Gesicht
Verscheucht von ihm den leichten Schlummer;
Er springt vom Rasen auf – er spricht:

Oedip
Ich träumte einen schweren Traum.
Schwang nicht den Zepter diese Rechte?
Doch Hoheit lös'ten starke Mächte
Dir auf, o Greis, in nicht'gen Schaum.

Trank ich in schönen Tagen nicht
In meiner großen Väter Halle,
Beym Heldensang und Hörnerschalle,
O Helios, dein golden Licht,

Das ich nun nimmer schauen kann?
Zerstörung ruft von allen Seiten:
"Zum Tode sollst du dich bereiten;
Dein irdisch Werk ist abgetan."

Schubert set this dramatic text in a throughcomposed form. The first three stanzas of Antigone's monologue, in which she prays for the gods' sympathy and observes her surroundings, are set as arioso. Each stanza has a distinct melody and accompanimental pattern and is written in a different key. After a short instrumental interlude mimicking the sighs and moans of the waking Oedipus, the fourth stanza adopts the bare texture of recitative. Here Antigone notices that her father has begun to stir. Oedipus' three stanzas, less cohesive than Antigone's, also involve no musical repetition. This second monologue is characterized initially by heroic triplet rhythms and C major harmonies, recalling the glories of Oedipus' past, and then by a solemn recitational vocal line, foretelling his fate. The throughcomposed form is well suited to the dramatic structure of the episode. Each dramatic moment, from Antigone's opening plea to Oedipus' premonition of death, requires individual musical expression. Repeating any musical section would undermine the mounting tension of the scene.

"Fahrt zum Hades" (D526), by contrast, is composed with a rounded form and consequently produces a very different effect. Mayrhofer's four-stanza poem depicts a metaphorical descent into hell:

> Der Nachen dröhnt, Cypressen flüstern –
> Horch, Geister reden schaurig drein;
> Bald werd' ich am Gestad', dem düstern,
> Weit von der schönen Erde sein.
>
> Da leuchten Sonne nicht, noch Sterne,
> Da tönt kein Lied, da ist kein Freund.
> Empfang die letzte Träne, o Ferne!
> Die dieses müde Auge weint.
>
> Schon schau' ich die blassen Danaiden,
> Den fluchbeladnen Tantalus;
> Es murmelt todesschwangern Frieden,
> Vergessenheit, dein alter Fluß.
>
> Vergessen nenn' ich zwiefach Sterben.
> Was ich mit höchster Kraft gewann,
> Verlieren – wieder es erwerben –
> Wann enden diese Qualen? Wann?

Significantly, Schubert repeats the first poetic stanza with nearly identical music at the end of the song. The large-scale musical form may thus be designated A B C D A. Despite the use of recitative in the fourth stanza (mm. 59–64), the song does not create an illusion of dramatic action. On the contrary, the musical/textual repetition suggests that the protagonist's situation at the end of the song does not differ from what it was at the beginning. The effect is closer to that of an aria or mixed-genre Lied than a dramatic scene. (Note that, contrary to the norm for the dramatic scene, the protagonist in this song is not named.) Because nothing "happens" in the course of the song, the text assumes a metaphorical quality, with the journey to Hades symbolizing the transition from life to death.

Progressive tonality is another means by which Schubert creates an illusion of dramatic action. Beginning and ending a song in different, often unrelated keys, produces an impression of change. In "Ganymed" (D544), to take just one example, Schubert depicts the protagonist's ascent into the heavens largely through harmonic modulation. The song begins in A♭ major, passes through a series of loosely related keys (E♭, C♭, G♭, E) in the various sections, and then finally concludes in F major. This open tonal structure, far from a compositional flaw, serves a clear interpretive purpose, illustrating action leading to Ganymede's apotheosis. (The piano postlude, ascending into the upper reaches of the keyboard, makes the nature of this dramatic event explicit.)

Dramatic scenes

Nearly half of Schubert's dramatic scenes begin and end in different keys, excluding modal shifts (see the list below). Many of these songs involve frequent changes of key (not to mention meter, tempo, and texture) throughout.

Dramatic scenes with open tonal structures

D5	Hagars Klage	c – A♭
D126	Szene aus Faust	C – B♭
D293	Shilrik und Vinvela	B♭ – A
D312	Hektors Abschied	f – A♭
D322	Hermann und Thusnelda	E♭ – B♭
D323	Klage der Ceres	G – B♭
D510	Didone abbandonata	E♭ – f
D544	Ganymed	A♭ – F
D545	Der Jüngling und der Tod	c♯ – B♭
D548	Orest auf Tauris	E♭ – D
D573	Iphigenia	G♭ – D♭
D674	Prometheus	g – C

Even those songs that begin and end in the same key are often highly chromatic and pass through many remote harmonic regions before returning to the original tonic. Here, too, a dramatic purpose is served.

Ex. 16 Schubert, "Szene aus Faust" (D126), 2nd version, mm. 51–54

56

Mise-en-scène

When the mise-en-scène, or physical location, for the action in a song is described, the dramatic effect becomes greatly enhanced. Sometimes the title or text provides clues to the location of the scene, thus bolstering the visual illusion. Occasionally the music too, through various kinds of text-painting, evokes an image of the physical setting in which the dramatic action ostensibly occurs.

"Szene aus Faust" is an excellent example. Goethe notes at the beginning of the scene that the action takes place within a cathedral. Significantly, Schubert adds this stage direction to the top of each of his manuscripts (both versions), suggesting that the listener should imagine the song as if it were performed on stage with a backdrop of stained-glass windows and choir stalls. Goethe's scene includes many references to the cathedral atmosphere: the evil spirit's mocking reminder of Gretchen's childhood visits to the altar, the chanting of the chorus, the stage direction "Orgelton", Gretchen's response to the music. Schubert's setting brings the cathedral atmosphere to life. Not only does he actualize Goethe's stage direction by composing "organ" music to accompany the choral verses, but he even strives for an occasional echo effect (Ex. 16).[16]

Other, somewhat less precise, musical indications of mise-en-scène in Schubert's dramatic scenes include the sounds of the stormy waves beating against the shores of Tauris in "Iphigenia" (Ex. 17) and the chirping of nightingales in the meadow, in "Ganymed" (Ex. 18). In each instance, musical text-painting intensifies the dramatic immediacy of the scene.

Dramatic Segment

Schubert's dramatic scenes typically depict a climactic episode from a famous story or myth. Rarely does a setting portray a complete subject, i.e., one with a definite beginning, middle, and end. Rather, the scene poses as an excerpted segment of a larger musico-dramatic work. It portrays only a small fragment of the full subject. To understand the song, the listener must recognize the dramatic context for the scene and imagine the missing parts.

An interesting consequence of the seemingly incomplete nature of dramatic scenes is the implication of a "before" and "after" time at either end of the song. Like many classical dramas, Schubert's dramatic scene texts frequently open *in medias res*, as if suddenly cutting in on dramatic action already in progress. Occasionally, as in "Orest auf Tauris" (D548), the musical setting supports this impression by beginning on non-tonic harmonies or with an abrupt modulation. The tonal ambiguity of the opening measures helps illustrate Orestes' initial confusion upon finding himself at the island of Tauris ("Ist dies Tauris?") (Ex. 19). One senses that the beginning of the song actually forms the continuation of previous, unheard music.

Ex. 17 Schubert, "Iphigenia" (D573), mm. 16–20

Ex. 18 Schubert, "Ganymed" (D544), mm. 61–67

Ex. 19 Schubert, "Orest auf Tauris" (D548), mm. 1–4

Dramatic scenes also typically conclude before the dramatic situation is resolved; the action ostensibly continues after the song has ended. But while many of Schubert's dramatic scenes have musically unstable beginnings, very few have unstable conclusions. None lacks a final cadence. "Verklärung" is a rare example of a song ending with a passage of recitative (a compositional practice generally frowned upon in Schubert's day), but even here there is an emphatic tonic cadence at the close (Ex. 20). The need for musical and especially tonal coherence, as defined by a song's ending, apparently outweighed dramatic considerations.

Ex. 20 Schubert, "Verklärung" (D59), mm. 38–41

Schubert's dramatic scenes, portraying identifiable personae engaged in action through the use of arioso and recitative, throughcomposed form, progressive tonal structures, illustrative accompaniments, and changing moods, stand in sharp contrast to the traditional strophic Lied. These were not, however, the only songs with dramatic characteristics. Many of the same traits are found in the dramatic ballad, to which we now turn our attention.

PART II

Dramatic ballads

4

The dramatic ballad tradition

Schubert's dramatic scenes are often confused with his dramatic ballads. In the Schubert literature, the names of these genres (and others, such as "cantata" and "monody") seem practically interchangeable. This confusion is not surprising, for the two kinds of song share many poetic and musical traits.

The similarities stem from the dramatic quality of the ballad's narrative mode. As we have noted, dramatic scenes have no narrators; their texts constitute direct speech by identifiable characters. While dramatic ballads do have narrators, the narrative mode is downplayed. The narrator injects himself as little as possible, rarely indulging in lengthy description, moralizing, or personal reflection on the characters, scene, or action. While nearly all ballad texts include narrative comment, dialogue is usually the central means of conveying the action of the story. Certain ballad texts are indeed constructed almost entirely from dialogue.[1] Thus the dramatic ballad "tends toward" the dramatic scene. The narration approaches pure drama. This dramatic tendency leads to musical settings closely resembling dramatic scenes.

Yet dramatic ballads display certain distinct characteristics as well and must be regarded as belonging to a separate genre. It is essential to recognize both the similarities and the differences between the dramatic ballad and related kinds of song.

Schubert's dramatic ballads date primarily from the mid-1810s and include settings of texts by a variety of poets.

Schubert's Dramatic Ballads

*also identifiable as mixed-genre Lieder

D7	Leichenfantasie (Schiller)	c 1811
D10	Der Vatermörder (Pfeffel)	1811
D77	Der Taucher (Schiller)	1813–14
D93/1–3	Don Gayseros (Fouqué)	1815?
D114	Romanze (Matthisson)	1814
D134	Ballade (Kenner)	c 1815
D144	Romanze, frag. (Stolberg)	1816
D149	Der Sänger (Goethe)	1815
D150	Lodas Gespenst (Ossian, trans. Harold)	1816

Dramatic ballads

D152	Minona (Bertrand)	1815
D166	Amphiaraos (Körner)	1815
D208, 212	Die Nonne (Hölty)	1815
D209	Der Liedler (Kenner)	1815
D211	Adelwold und Emma (Bertrand)	1815
D246	Die Bürgschaft (Schiller)	1815
D327, 376	Lorma, frag. (Ossian, trans. Harold)	1815, 1816
D328	* Erlkönig (Goethe)	1815
D329	Die drei Sänger, frag. (Bobrik)	1815
D375	Der Tod Oscars (Ossian, trans. Harold)	1816
D397	Ritter Toggenburg (Schiller)	1816
D473	Liedesend (Mayrhofer)	1816
D554	Uraniens Flucht (Mayrhofer)	1817
D702	Der Jüngling auf dem Hügel (Hüttenbrenner)	1820
D728	Johanna Sebus, frag. (Goethe)	1821
D771	* Der Zwerg (Collin)	1822 or 1823
D786	* Viola (Schober)	1823
D792	* Vergißmeinnicht (Schober)	1823

These songs are throughcomposed settings of poetic texts in which the words and actions of a small group of identifiable characters are related by an anonymous narrator.[2] Each ballad focuses on a single crucial episode, with no subplots or other distractions. The narration begins abruptly at a point in the story where the action is clearly headed toward some sort of catastrophe. One event leads to the next until the climax is reached. The narrative then ends as suddenly as it began.

To convey the action of the story, Schubert uses sectional musical forms comprising passages of recitative, arioso, and Lied-like melodies, as well as meandering harmonic schemes and frequent text-painting. Because their narratives relate a series of actions or events, Schubert's dramatic ballads are much longer than most Lieder, extending to as many as thirty pages of music.

At the outset, the dramatic ballad must be distinguished from another type of narrative song: the strophic ballad. Although both are often simply designated "ballad" on account of their narrative, stanzaic texts, they clearly represent very different kinds of song.

Strophic ballads possess the repetitive musical structure and general character of Volkslieder. Simple, unadorned melodies with balanced phrasing and plain chordal or patterned accompaniments help create an impression of spontaneity and artlessness, as if the singer were reviving a centuries-old tune. A good example is "Der König in Thule" (D367), whose ballad text originally appeared in Part I, scene viii of Goethe's *Faust*. In the play, the ballad is sung by Gretchen after her first encounter with Faust. The melancholic tale of the medieval king who lost his true love serves an important dramatic function by foreshadowing Gretchen's own desolation. Schubert's strophic setting mimics the sound of medieval balladry with its square chordal accompaniment, rhythmic simplicity, and aura of modality, resulting from the use of the dominant minor and the lack of seventh chords. One can easily imagine Gretchen singing this plain, unpretentious melody to the accompaniment of a lute or guitar.

Other strophic ballads by Schubert include "Das Mädchen aus der Fremde" (D117), "Lieb Minna" (D222), "Der Fischer" (D225), "Die Spinnerin" (D247), "Der Gott und die Bajadere" (D254), "Der Schatzgräber" (D256), "Heiden-röslein" (D257), and "Eine altschottische Ballade" (D923). Most of these songs have texts by Goethe and were set to music in 1815 – the same year that Schubert composed the majority of his dramatic ballad settings. Their subjects are primarily pastoral or domestic, involving sentimental rather than dramatic incidents. The stories, like that of "Heidenröslein," often have a timeless, universal quality, as if the narrated sequence of events were but one instance of an endlessly recurring historical pattern: that which has happened once will happen many times again. The strophic musical repetitions support this impression. Significantly, strophic ballads generally do not identify their characters by name, as do dramatic ballads. Instead, the characters are presented as types – a medieval king, a fisherman, a maiden, a mother. Identifying characters by name particularizes, i.e. dramatizes, the situation, weakening the impression of universality.

While the dramatic ballad differs markedly from the strophic ballad, it bears close resemblance to yet another type of narrative song: the Romanze. In the early decades of the nineteenth century, the terms *Ballade* and *Romanze* were used nearly synonymously.[3] Certain small differences were recognized. The Romanze, originating in Spain, had a lyrical, light-hearted character, drawing upon themes of love and chivalry. The ballad, originating in the northern lands of England, Scotland, and Germany, possessed a more serious tone and involved legendary, historical, and mystical subjects. By Schubert's day, however, the two traditions had essentially merged.

The close relation between the two types of song becomes apparent through a brief comparison of two Schubert Lieder: "Romanze" (D114) and "Ballade" (D134). In "Romanze," a setting of a Matthisson poem dating from 1791, a young maiden locked in a dark tower by her evil uncle laments her misfortune before eventually dying of grief and loneliness. Matthisson's poem, "Ein Fräulein in Thurme: Romanze," inspired Schubert's friend Josef Kenner to compose similar verse of his own. Kenner's "Ein Fräulein schaut vom hohen Turm" tells a related story. A young girl imprisoned in a tower gazes out to sea for the hero who will rescue her; he arrives but is soon slain in battle; the maiden strews roses over his body and is then herself murdered. Schubert gave his setting of Kenner's poem the title "Ballade."

Both "Romanze" and "Ballade" exhibit typical features of dramatic ballad composition, including recitative, text-painting, mostly throughcomposed sectional forms, and the repeated quarter note–eighth note rhythmic pattern conventionally known as the "Romanzenton" (Ex. 21a and 21b). "Romanze," however, has a more remote, story-book quality, arising from its lack of

Ex. 21a Schubert, "Romanze" (D114), mm. 1–5

dialogue, rounded musical form (the opening section repeats at the end), and fewer key changes. The difference is one of tone. "Ballade" presents its narrative in stark dramatic terms; "Romanze" balances drama with lyricism. Nevertheless, the two songs belong to the same general category of composition, their similarities far outweighing their differences. For our purposes, the Romanze may usefully be considered a subset of the dramatic ballad, rather than a separate genre.

Schubert was hardly the first composer to write dramatic ballads. By the early 1810s, when he made his initial experiments with this type of song setting, a tradition of ballad composition had been in existence for nearly thirty-five years.

The earliest musical settings of German ballad texts were strophic, resembling Volkslieder. Among the first songs based on Gottfried August Bürger's famous ballad "Lenore" (written in 1773), for example, were strophic settings by Friedrich Wilhelm Weis (1776), Georg Wilhelm Gruber (1780), Johann Philipp Kirnberger (1780), and George Friedrich Wolf (1781). Similarly, both Siegmund Freiherr von Seckendorff (1779) and Joseph Anton Steffan (1782) composed strophic settings of the Scottish folk ballad "Edward."

Strophic form was a natural choice for ballad settings because the texts were nearly always stanzaic. Before long, however, composers began to recognize the advantages of throughcomposition for conveying the dramatic essence of these poetic narratives.[4] In rejecting the principle of strophic repetition,

The dramatic ballad tradition

Ex. 21b Schubert, "Ballade" (D134), mm. 1–5

Mäßig geschwind

Ein Fräu-lein schaut _ vom ho-hen Thurm das wei-te Meer _ so bang, zum

composers essentially created a new genre, allied not with Volkslieder but with dramatic vocal genres such as the operatic scene and melodrama.[5]

This transformation is noted by Heinrich Christoph Koch in his *Musikalisches Lexikon* of 1802:[6]

> The melody of a ballad, whose character is determined by the subject matter of the poem, is not bound to a particular form or meter. For some time now, people have begun to throughcompose the text entirely, rather than repeat the music for each strophe of the text, as with the Lied.

Curiously, Koch gives no reason for this change in compositional technique; he says nothing about the dramatic musical effect of throughcomposition.

Comparison of the full 1802 ballad definition, however, with the revised version published in the *Kurzgefaßtes Handwörterbuch* of 1807 suggests that Koch came to perceive the dramatic essence of the ballad. In the 1802 definition, Koch describes the ballad as:[7]

> [a] type of song covering many strophes of a poem whose primary subject is love and which, because it was originally danced and sung, had a suitably measured verse. . . .
>
> Our modern ballads differ little from the romances and, because they are merely intended to be sung, require a lyrical meter.

Here, the ballad is conceived as a lyrical love song with a stanzaic text. No mention is made of any narrative structure in the poem. In Koch's 1807 definition, the ballad is described quite differently:[8]

> Ballad signifies a very distinct and characteristic type of poetry. It is a story of an event that is either adventurous, wondrous, gruesome, tragi-comic, or all of these together. Love is always involved, although the story need not be about the love between unmarried persons.
>
> Although the ballad is not a lyrical poem, it is nevertheless intended to be sung.

This revised formulation stresses the non-lyrical quality of the ballad. Now the ballad is viewed as a narrative song relating a suspenseful episode.

Koch concludes the 1807 definition with the same off-hand reference to throughcomposition that appears at the end of the 1802 definition. Within the context of the 1807 definition, this reference becomes meaningful. Narrative texts with Sturm und Drang subjects, in which suspense mounts until the denouement, clearly require non-repetitive musical settings.

The earliest throughcomposed German ballad was a setting of "Lenore" composed in 1775 by Johann André, a Singspiel composer and publisher working primarily in Offenbach am Main and Berlin.[9] An immediate success, the work played a crucial role in establishing the conventions of the genre. Soon after the appearance of the first edition of the song, André wrote several new versions. The first and second versions were composed for solo voice and piano. The third version, by contrast, was composed for four solo voices, chorus, and orchestra, with a pronounced dramatic effect. The soprano, alto, and bass solos sing the parts of Lenore, her mother, and Wilhelm; as in a Passion oratorio, the tenor solo assumes the role of a narrator. The fourth version, while written mostly for solo voice and piano, seems modeled after the third in that it retains the choral parts and features a richer, orchestral-sounding accompaniment.

All of the versions, but most notably the first, comprise a succession of closed strophes corresponding to the poetic stanzas. Occasionally, where the meaning of various poetic stanzas is similar, André repeats a musical strophe; otherwise the settings are throughcomposed. The musical texture embraces Lied-like melodies as well as recitative and arioso passages. While in the early versions of the song the accompaniment does little more than provide harmonic support for the voice, in the later versions it helps illustrate the story's unfolding drama through text-painting.

Friedrich Ludwig Aemilius Kunzen, a prolific composer of dramatic music at Copenhagen, Berlin, Frankfurt, and Prague, published a through-composed setting of "Lenore" for voice and piano in 1788. Subtitled "ein musikalisches Gemälde," Kunzen's setting combines elements of song and melodrama. Only those parts of Bürger's text which constitute direct speech are actually sung. The narrative sections are either declaimed (against a musical background or without accompaniment) or read silently. The work betrays the strong influence of Benda's melodramas, which were then much in vogue.

Another "Lenore" setting, with yet greater dramatic effect, was completed in 1805 or 1806 by the Czech composer Wenzel Johann Tomaschek. Written for solo voice and piano, this ballad setting far exceeds the usual proportions of song composition. It begins with a 210-measure overture, comprising both a slow introduction and a fast sonata movement. The full song encompasses fifty-one oblong folios in the original manuscript. Given its tremendous scope, Tomaschek's setting not surprisingly has little in common with traditional Lieder; the influence of operatic styles is evident throughout. Rather than alternating between contrasting musical textures, as do most throughcomposed ballads, Tomaschek's "Lenore" constitutes a series of closed melodic sections, resembling a chain of operatic arias.

In 1797, Johann Rudolf Zumsteeg, the principal ballad composer before Karl Loewe, wrote the most famous setting of "Lenore." Like Zumsteeg's other throughcomposed ballads, the work displays the strong influence of both melodrama and opera, particularly that of Gluck.[10] The musical setting depicts a succession of sharp visual images: the celebratory march of the soldiers, Lenore's heart-wrenching lament, Wilhelm's mysterious arrival, and the midnight ghost-ride. To convey the essence of the story, Zumsteeg engages in elaborate text-painting (e.g., unison textures for Wilhelm's ghost voice, 6/8 meter for the night ride, piano tremolos for the arrival at the grave).

"Lenore" was one of six large ballad settings that Zumsteeg composed during the last decade of his life and that were published as independent works:[11]

Des Pfarrers Tochter von Taubenhayn (Bürger)	1790/91
Die Entführung (Bürger)	1793/94
Die Büßende (Stolberg)	1796/97
Lenore (Bürger)	1797/98
Elwine (von Ulmenstein)	1801/01
Das Lied von Treue, frag. (Bürger)	1801

In addition, Zumsteeg composed a number of shorter throughcomposed ballads, which appeared in the seven volumes of *Kleine Balladen und Lieder* (1800–05):[12]

Ritter Toggenburg (Schiller)
Robert und Käthe (Werthes)
Richard und Mathilde (Haug)
Des Mädchens Klage (Schiller)
Die beiden Bonzen (Pfeffel)

These songs were well known by Zumsteeg's contemporaries and frequently performed in private salons and public concerts through the 1840s. The numerous reviews of his ballads (as well as those by Kunzen, Tomaschek, and other composers) that appeared in music journals such as the Leipzig

Allgemeine musikalische Zeitung help substantiate the wide appeal of dramatic ballads during the early nineteenth century.[13]

While Schubert was probably familiar with the dramatic songs of many composers, Zumsteeg's appear to have influenced him most. Several of Schubert's close friends – Anton Holzapfel, Josef Kenner, and Joseph von Spaun – later recalled that he developed a keen interest in Zumsteeg's songs during his early years at the Vienna Stadtkonvikt.[14] In his obituary notice "On Schubert" (1829), Spaun remarks:[15]

> Schubert was extremely well versed in the classical works of the great masters. For Handel, Gluck, Mozart, Haydn and Beethoven he felt an enthusiastic reverence. Zumsteeg's songs, with which he became acquainted already as a boy and which specially appealed to him, may have had some influence on his predilection for German song, which began to develop so early.

Zumsteeg's songs were great favorites within Schubert's musical circle at the Stadtkonvikt. Holzapfel reminisces that "little coteries, willingly condoned by the Director, were formed for the performance of string and vocal quartets; songs at the pianoforte, especially the ballads and songs of Zumsteeg, also became very popular with us."[16] Sometimes Schubert played and sang both parts himself. Other times classmates, such as Albert Stadler and Holzapfel, performed the piano and vocal parts while Schubert and the rest listened.

In his memoirs, Spaun mentions several songs by Zumsteeg that Schubert encountered in his student days:[17]

> [Spring 1811] After some days I went to see him [Schubert] in the music room where he was given an hour for practice. He had several of Zumsteeg's songs in front of him and told me that these songs moved him profoundly. "Listen," he said once, "to the song I have here" and with a voice already half breaking he sang "Kolma"; then he showed me "Erwartung," ("Maria Stuart"), "Ritter Toggenburg" etc. He said he could revel in these songs for days on end. And to this youthful predilection of his we probably owe the direction Schubert took, and yet how little of an imitator he was and how independent the path he followed.
>
> He had already at that time attempted a few songs, for example, Hagars Klage. He wanted to modernize Zumsteeg's song form, which very much appealed to him.

Of the songs referred to by Spaun, "Ritter Toggenburg," "Die Erwartung," and "Maria Stuart" were all published in the first three volumes of Zumsteeg's *Kleine Balladen und Lieder*. Presumably, then, Schubert was familiar with the contents of these initial volumes, if not also the remaining four. Zumsteeg's settings of "Kolma" and "Hagars Klage" were published independently, as were "Iglous, der Mohrin Klagegesang" and the six large ballads. Schubert apparently had access to some of these works as well.

The dramatic ballad tradition

Several of Schubert's early dramatic songs appear to be modeled directly on Zumsteeg's settings of the same texts. Such is the case, for example, with "Hagars Klage" (D5), which Spaun refers to as Schubert's "earliest song composition, written at the Konvikt at the age of fourteen." Not only does Schubert adopt the older composer's solo cantata form, with its loose alternation of recitative and arioso, but he also imitates the general sequence of tempo changes demarcating different sections. Thus where Zumsteeg's sections are successively headed "Langsam," "Rasch," "Langsam," "Geschwind," etc., the corresponding textual passages in Schubert's setting are marked "Largo," "Allegro," "Largo," "Geschwind." Schubert's "Die Erwartung" (D159) and "Ritter Toggenburg" (D397), both composed in 1816, also appear to be modeled directly upon Zumsteeg's settings. In the latter song, Schubert follows Zumsteeg in switching from throughcomposition to strophic form for stanzas 6–9 of Schiller's poem.

But these early songs are not slavish imitations. As Gunter Maier has demonstrated, Schubert's songs reflect a desire to improve upon the original.[18] When Schubert deviates from Zumsteeg's compositional model, he generally does so in a way that permits greater fidelity to the meaning of the text. Spaun's statement that Schubert "wanted to modernize Zumsteeg's song form" indicates that his friend was not content simply to copy the dramatic songs of his predecessors. Rather he hoped to renovate the tradition.

5

An example of Schubert's dramatic ballads

"Der Taucher" (D77)

The magnificent setting of "Der Taucher" (D77) (which was not, incidentally, modeled after any setting by Zumsteeg) shows dramatic ballad composition near its best. Schubert composed two versions of the song. The first he began on September 17, 1813 and finished on April 5, 1814. The second, also begun in September 1813, was completed in August 1814, then amended at the beginning of the following year. For Schubert to work concurrently on two versions of a song was unusual. The significant amount of energy and time that he devoted to "Der Taucher" attests to his fascination with the genre. The many changes incorporated into the second version bespeak a desire to capture in music the delicate balance of drama and narrative in the text.[1]

Schiller's twenty-seven-stanza poem (translation on pp. 142–145) stands in sharp contrast to the Sturm und Drang ballads of his predecessors, whose gruesome tragedies and lurid tales of violated love accentuate the horrific, the maudlin, and the bizarre.[2] "Der Taucher," like most of Schiller's ballads, is an "Ideenballade," intended to teach a moral lesson. The poem warns of the dangers of intellectual greed, of questing for knowledge beyond human capacity. A king, driven by an insatiable curiosity and a certain masochism, dares any of his subjects to fetch a golden chalice he has thrown into the seething waters of a whirlpool that lies below the cliff where they stand. When none of his knights accepts the challenge, a young squire steps forward and dives into the tumultuous sea. After a tension-filled interval, the youth reappears at the surface, proudly waving the cup. Greeted by joyous cheers from the crowd, he returns the chalice to the king and tells a harrowing tale of his perilous descent into the black, raging waters, his good fortune of spying the cup suspended on a tip of coral, and his timely escape from the monsters of the deep. When the king learns that the youth never penetrated the utmost depths of the watery hell, he hurls the cup back into the water, renewing the challenge with promise of an additional reward. The king's daughter protests against her father's cruelty, but this merely inspires the king to offer her hand in marriage if the youth can retrieve the cup again. The youth, inflamed by love, dives a second time off the cliff, and is seen no more.

The narrative begins precipitously, with the king's initial challenge, and presses ahead without distraction to the climax in the final line. There are no subplots or extraneous descriptions of setting or character to slow the pace. The only repetition of text, involving the first three lines of stanzas 6 and 12, furthers rather than impedes the dramatic action.[3] Whereas in stanza 6 the lines (which focus attention on the seething waters) have a descriptive function, in stanza 12 they help to build tension as the crowd awaits the return of the youth. Contributing to the momentum is the additive construction of the verse. In the third through sixth stanzas, for example, as many as half of the twenty-four lines begin with the word "und".

Although the poem is organized in regular six-line stanzas, with a consistent stress pattern (434444) and rhyme scheme (ababcc) maintained throughout, the action of the narrative follows its own course, frequently obscuring the external form. One discrepancy between narrative content and stanzaic structure occurs in the fourth stanza:

> Doch alles noch stumm bleibt wie zuvor,
> Und ein Edelknecht, sanft und keck,
> Tritt aus der Knappen zagendem Chor,
> Und den Gürtel wirft er, den Mantel weg,
> Und alle die Männer umher und Frauen
> Auf den herrlichen Jüngling verwundert schauen.

With regard to subject, the first line of this stanza belongs with the previous three stanzas; it forms part of the opening segment of the narrative which relates the king's challenge and the nervous silence that follows. The next stage of the narrative begins with the appearance of the youth in the second line of the fourth stanza. This important event does not coincide with the beginning of a stanza, indeed does not even occur at the start of a sentence.

Throughout the poem, the narrator's identity remains hidden. But because the narrative unfolds in the present tense, Schiller creates the impression that the narrator is one of the crowd on the cliff, watching the action in person. Exclamations, such as that which begins stanza 13, sustain this impression:

> Und sieh! aus dem finster flutenden Schoß
> Da hebet sich's schwanenweiß,
> Und ein Arm und ein glänzender Nacken wird bloß,
> Und es rudert mit Kraft und mit emsigem Fleiß,
> Und er ist's, und hoch in seiner Linken
> Schwingt er den Becher mit freudigem Winken.

Similarly, the only time the narrator exposes his own emotions (in an aside to the reader/listener in stanza 10, shortly after the youth has taken the first plunge), his ostensible fear places him in the position of those tremulous onlookers who refused the king's challenge.

Dramatic ballads

Und wärfst du die Krone selber hinein
Und sprächst: wer mir bringet die Kron',
Er soll sie tragen und König sein –
Mich gelüstete nicht nach dem teuren Lohn.
Was die heulende Tiefe da unten verhehle,
Das erzählt keine lebende glückliche Seele.

Present tense narration, like the inclusion of dialogue, heightens the illusion of drama, of characters enacting a series of events before our eyes. Significantly, the mixture of dialogue and narrative comment in "Der Taucher" may be interpreted in either of two ways. One might regard the narrator as quoting the direct speech of the various characters. According to this conventional view, the narrator has complete control of the story – its length, details, direction, and outcome. He tells his tale in the present tense so as better to grip his audience. Alternatively, one may imagine the narrator as "sharing the stage" with the characters in his story, in the manner of the testo in an oratorio. On this interpretation, the narrator's role is reduced to that of an eyewitness reporter. Schiller's poem exploits the ambiguity to achieve both narrative control and dramatic effect.

In Schubert's second version of "Der Taucher," the dramatic illusion created by the text is bolstered by an array of compositional techniques. To vivify the different characters, he sets their lines in contrasting styles, capturing the distinctive aspects of their personalities. The sharp dotted rhythms, octave doublings (new to the second version), and forte dynamic of the chords that introduce the king's first recitative signal his power and royalty. Schubert evidently also wished to underscore the king's essential cruelty, for in early 1815 he rewrote his last speech, substituting harsh fortissimo chords for what had been a quiet and sparsely written accompanimental passage. The bold nature of the youth is conveyed by the abrupt key change from C to A♭ at mm. 69ff, the large vocal leaps, and accentuated sustained chords in the piano part. To depict the gentle manner of the king's daughter, Schubert surrounds her recitative with lyrical arioso passages, constructed from a repeated accompanimental pattern (mm. 452–469). The graceful octave leaps, flowing eighth-note rhythms, predominantly stepwise vocal line, and piano dynamic together create an aural impression of feminine charm. Interestingly, the narrator's lines are not set in a distinctive way and consequently do not conjure an image of his character. His music changes in accordance with the events of his story.

At the beginning of the song, Schubert sets the words of the king as an accompanied recitative. He then switches to an arioso texture with the entrance of the narrator in the second stanza. This contrast in texture helps the listener identify the different personae, a task made difficult by the fact that there is only one singer. The ballad does not, however, maintain a strict relation between direct speech and recitative on the one hand, and narrative comment and arioso on the other. Although all of the king's lines are delivered in recitative, those of his daughter and the youth are presented in a mixture of declamatory and lyrical styles. Moreover, the narrator occasionally uses recitative, as, for example, at the end of the third stanza, where he introduces the king's third query (mm. 57–58) and throughout the eighth, where he describes the youth's plunge. But while there is no strict correspondence between type of speech and musical texture, changes of texture are an important means by which Schubert highlights changes of speaker. Rhythm, meter, tempo, key, dynamics, and articulation (though not register, as in "Erlkönig") also play a significant role.

Schubert's use of an essentially throughcomposed musical form helps convey the action of the narrative. Just as the story pushes toward its conclusion, with each poetic stanza furthering the action, so does the music. The only musical repetition of substantial length occurs in mm. 215–230, which essentially duplicate mm. 112–127; as noted, the two passages have nearly identical texts (stanzas 6 and 12). (A second shorter, though more significant, instance of musical repetition will be discussed below.) The stanzaic structure of the poem is obscured by the on-running musical form.

To portray the turn of events in the story, Schubert makes use of frequent and often surprising modulations. When the youth first steps forward to accept the king's challenge, the key shifts abruptly from C major to A♭ major (mm. 65–69). The change of key draws attention to this important new stage of the narrative. In this instance, Schubert writes a closed fourteen-measure period, beginning and ending in A♭ major. Through most of the setting, however, the musical sections modulate through a succession of keys, often leading to new dominant harmonies that press ahead in unsuspected directions. Such is the case with Schubert's setting of stanza 5, which moves through g minor, B♭ major, c minor, and d minor, before finally landing on the dominant of c minor.

Schubert also makes frequent use of text-painting to depict the course of the action and the physical setting of the story. In m. 9, when the king hurls the chalice into the raging sea, Schubert writes a descending arpeggio in the piano accompaniment that illustrates the trajectory of the cup (Ex. 22). In m. 257, when the youth appears at the surface of the water holding up the cup for all to see, Schubert captures the gesture with an octave leap in the vocal part (Ex. 23). The whirlpool is depicted in a number of passages throughout the song. For this central image, Schubert's arsenal includes piano tremolos (Ex. 24a), ascending sixteenth-note runs (Ex. 24b, here specifically illustrating the "regurgitation" of water), and swirling accompanimental patterns (Ex. 24c).

Schubert's desire to emphasize the dramatic aspects of the ballad text is evident in various changes he made in the second version of the song. Besides creating a stricter separation of recitative and arioso and improving the declamation of certain vocal passages, Schubert also made a number of

Ex. 22 Schubert, "Der Taucher" (D77), 2nd version, mm. 8–9

Ex. 23 Schubert, "Der Taucher" (D77), 2nd version, mm. 254–262

significant alterations to the piano accompaniment. In some places, such as mm. 41 and 436–437, he inserted new measures of rests. Elsewhere, he added segments of accompanimental music ranging from one to fifty-nine measures, and rewrote existing passages. The effect of many of these changes is to heighten the dramatic illusion, that is, to put the listener in the position of an eyewitness to the scene. This is clearly the intention of the lengthy accompanimental interlude that Schubert inserted prior to the last stanza. Here the listener himself experiences the interminable wait for the

An example of Schubert's dramatic ballads

Ex. 24a Schubert, "Der Taucher" (D77), 2nd version, mm. 5–6

Ex. 24b Schubert, "Der Taucher" (D77), 2nd version, mm. 95–99

return of the youth after his second dive. Narrative time has expanded to approach dramatic time. The same is true on a smaller scale of the instrumental interlude in mm. 65–68, which follows the narrator's line "Doch alles noch stumm bleibt wie zuvor"; the listener is allowed to "hear" the crowd's silence (Ex. 25). In both of these instances, Schubert makes explicit what is implicit in Schiller's text: a tension-filled interval of waiting.

Dramatic ballads

Ex. 24c Schubert, "Der Taucher" (D77), 2nd version, mm. 112–115

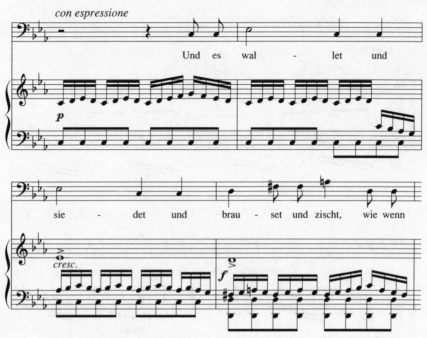

Ex. 25 Schubert, "Der Taucher" (D77), 2nd version, mm. 63–69

An example of Schubert's dramatic ballads

"Der Taucher" is not, however, a straightforward dramatic rendering of the episode, but rather a narrative. Certain aspects of the song derive directly from the narrative mode of presentation. Most obviously, the song involves a narrator who, as noted, may be understood as either quoting the other characters or sharing the stage with them. Both interpretations permit the narrator a degree of control over how the story unfolds, and in several instances the subject is manipulated in ways that would not be possible in a dramatic scene. In stanza 10, for example, the narrator foreshadows the tragic ending of the song: "Was die heulende Tiefe da unten verhehle,/Das erzählte keine lebende glückliche Seele." Interestingly, in the second version of the song, Schubert places less emphasis on these lines. Whereas in the first version, he sets them in a lyrical arioso lasting seventeen measures (mm. 185–201) and repeats the second line so as to underscore its significance, in the second version he compresses the passage to a five-measure recitative (mm. 192–196) and omits the text repetition. While he downplays this passage, he inserts another whose function is also to foreshadow the tragic ending. The descending chromatic bass line of the piano accompaniment in mm. 53–55 (not included in the first version), which immediately follows the narrator's description of the silence induced by the king's challenge, anticipates the doom that awaits any who dares to step forward (Ex. 26).

Ex. 26 Schubert, "Der Taucher" (D77), 2nd version, mm. 49–56

Ex. 27 Schubert, "Der Taucher" (D77), 2nd version, mm. 164–167

The narrator also manipulates the story by retelling certain crucial events. Just as the textual repetition in stanzas 6 and 12 inspires a musical repetition, so does the narrator's retelling of the king's act of throwing the chalice into the sea. In mm. 8–9, the king announces, "Einen goldnen Becher werf ich hinab." As noted, Schubert then writes a descending accompanimental arpeggio to illustrate the motion of the cup. In mm. 22–24, when the narrator retells the event ("Der König spricht es und wirft von der Höh der Klippe. . ."), Schubert uses the same musical gesture.

A more significant (though differently inspired) musical repetition occurs near the end of the song when the king once again tosses the chalice off the cliff. Measures 472–479 ("Drauf der König greift nach dem Becher schnell, in den Strudel ihn schleudert hinein") are an almost exact repeat of mm. 17–24, the narrator's retelling of the king's announcement. The musical repetition at the end of the song does not arise from the narrator's retelling of a single event but rather from the structural symmetry of the tale. The ballad begins and ends with the king throwing the cup into the water. The repetition of this act inspires the musical repetition.

Just as the narrator repeats certain parts of the story, so he omits others. In Schiller's poem, the youth's first dive is never actually mentioned by the narrator. The event evidently takes place during the dash in the third line of stanza 8:

An example of Schubert's dramatic ballads

> Jetzt schnell, eh' die Brandung wiederkehrt,
> Der Jüngling sich Gott befiehlt,
> Und – ein Schrei des Entsetzens wird rings gehört,
> Und schon hat ihn der Wirbel hinweggespült,
> Und geheimnisvoll über dem kühnen Schwimmer
> Schließt sich der Rachen, er zeigt sich nimmer.

In Schubert's setting, this crucial event is also missing. The fortissimo diminished chord in the piano accompaniment of m. 166 sounds the cry that goes up from the crowd (Ex. 27).

The narrative mode of the text also helps to account for the tremendous length of the song – 605 measures. Unlike dramatic scenes, which portray climactic segments of usually well-known subjects, "Der Taucher" tells a complete story, with beginning, middle, and end. The complexity of the narrative, with its multiple personae and sequence of events, results in a poem of twenty-seven stanzas and nearly thirty minutes of music.

The use of a complete poetic subject in this musical narrative also has important implications for the beginning and ending of the song. Schubert opens the setting with a half-cadence in the key of d minor – an abrupt and unsettling musical gesture reflecting the nature of the king's challenge. Almost immediately, the harmony shifts away from d minor and wanders through a series of loosely related keys. Throughout the song, the tonal center continues to wander, with no clear organizational principle. At the beginning of the long piano interlude that precedes the final stanza, however, Schubert returns to d minor, and he concludes the song solidly in that key. The sixty-two measure piano interlude bears some resemblance to a cadenza in that it grants extra weight to the final cadence. Notwithstanding the weak harmonic beginning, the tremendous length of the setting, and the numerous key changes throughout, the resolution in d minor gives a sense of roundedness to the song. This impression, supported by the brief repetition of music from stanza 2 in stanza 25, parallels the complete nature of the poetic subject. Just as the narrator rounds his tale into a unified whole, so does Schubert.

In sum, "Der Taucher" combines dramatic and narrative elements. Surely both the riveting excitement of dramatic immediacy and the subtle complexities of story-telling accounted for much of the ballad's popularity in Schubert's day.

6

Poetic and musical traits of the dramatic ballad

As with the dramatic scene, the many individual traits that identify the dramatic ballad coalesce into several principal characteristics: (1) setting of a narrative text for solo voice and piano, (2) simulation of drama, (3) evidence of narrative control, (4) representation of a complete story. Not all dramatic ballads display every characteristic. Some songs clearly belong to the genre while others lie on the periphery. On the whole, however, Schubert's dramatic ballads form a fairly cohesive group. The problematic songs are few.

Narrative Text

The majority of Schubert's dramatic ballads use texts that are themselves identifiable as ballads. The narrative, stanzaic poems imitate the style, structure, and subjects of folk balladry. Although not actually part of an oral tradition, the poems reflect the widespread interest in folk poetry that gained currency in the 1770s and after.[1]

Perhaps the most salient feature of the ballad texts is their narrative mode. Ballads tell stories. Almost without exception, the stories are told from a third person point of view. The anonymous narrator does not participate in the events of the tale. His emotions are concealed, making the narrative descriptive rather than introspective.[2]

Most of Schubert's ballad texts comprise a mixture of narrative comment and dialogue. As noted in the analysis of "Der Taucher," the mixture suggests two possible interpretations: the narrator may be quoting the speech of the characters, or sharing the stage with them.[3] The latter interpretation naturally seems most plausible when the story is told in the present tense.

The proportions of narrative comment and dialogue vary widely from work to work. In some ballads, there is no dialogue, or virtually none. Such is the case with "Leichenfantasie" (D7), "Don Gayseros III" (D93/3), "Romanze" (D114), "Ballade" (D134), "Die Nonne" (D208, 212), "Ritter Toggenburg" (D397), "Der Jüngling auf dem Hügel" (D702), "Viola" (D786), and "Vergißmeinnicht" (D792). "Don Gayseros I" (D93/1), on the other hand, consists almost entirely of dialogue; only the last of the fourteen stanzas is spoken directly by the narrator. Similarly, just two of the eight stanzas in

"Erlkönig" (D328) belong unequivocally to the narrator.[4] The remaining ballads fall somewhere in between these two extremes. In general, the greater the amount of dialogue, the closer the link to a dramatic mode of expression.

Creating an illusion of drama is central to the ballad's aesthetics. Besides using dialogue, this is often accomplished by present tense narration. Examples of dramatic ballads told in the present tense include "Don Gayseros III" (D93/3), "Minona" (D152), "Liedesend" (D473), "Uraniens Flucht" (D554), and "Viola" (D786). Even in songs without dialogue, present-tense narration heightens the illusion of dramatic action. The reader/listener is encouraged to believe that the events of the story are taking place at that very moment. The narrator's role thus seems reduced to that of an eyewitness reporter, not creating the events and characters of his story but merely describing them.

Sometimes the narrative unfolds in a combination of past and present tense, as in "Leichenfantasie" (D7), "Der Taucher" (D77), "Ballade" (D134), "Lodas Gespenst" (D150), "Minona" (D152), "Amphiaraos" (D166), "Die Nonne" (D208, 212), "Adelwold und Emma" (D211), "Erlkönig" (D328), and "Der Tod Oscars" (D375). In nearly every case, the present tense intensifies the dramatic illusion, while the past tense has a distancing effect.

In ballad texts composed entirely in the past tense, such as "Der Vatermörder" (D10), "Der Sänger" (D149), and "Ritter Toggenburg" (D397), the narrator's role appears strengthened. An interval of time separates the story's events from the world of the audience, thus emphasizing the narrator's controlling hand. The same, of course, holds true for ballads which slip into the future tense. In "Der Zwerg" (D771), for example, nearly the entire story is related in the present tense, suggesting that not even the narrator knows how it will conclude. Suspense mounts, until suddenly in the last line, the narrator foretells the dwarf's fate: "An keiner Küste wird er je mehr landen." The abrupt introduction of the future tense suggests the narrator's omniscience.

In sum, most of Schubert's dramatic ballad texts employ a mode of expression with both narrative and dramatic aspects. The narrator's presence is sometimes obvious and sometimes obscure, but always detectable. At the same time, nearly every song creates an illusion of drama through the use of dialogue and/or the present tense. This combination of narrative and dramatic qualities has important implications for the musical settings.

The external structures of Schubert's dramatic ballad texts are fairly uniform. Except for the Ossian songs, whose texts are written in prose, all of the dramatic ballads have regular stanzaic texts with many characteristics of folk poetry. The stanzas, ranging from one to forty in number and averaging about nine, generally comprise either four or eight lines with the rhyme scheme abab, ababcdcd, or some close variation.[5] Most of the ballads have an accentuation pattern with either four stressed syllables per line, or a combination of four and three stressed syllables.[6] Meter is also remarkably consistent. The majority of the texts are composed in strict iambic meter, a somewhat smaller number in trochaic meter.[7]

Dramatic ballads

The Ossian texts, written in prose, differ markedly from the other ballads. Indeed, there may be disagreement as to whether "Lodas Gespenst" (D150), "Lorma," frag. (D327, 376), and "Der Tod Oscars" (D375) should even be considered dramatic ballads. An argument might be made that Schubert's Ossian settings – those with narrative as well as dramatic texts – form a unique category of song, so distinctive are their linguistic style, structure, and subject.

While this perspective has some merit, there is good reason to group some of the Ossian songs with Schubert's dramatic ballads. The throughcomposed musical settings of dramatic ballads tend to obscure the stanzaic outlines of the texts. The use of recitative and arioso hides the regularity of stress, meter, and rhyme. Indeed, the external structure of the text has far less bearing on the musical setting than the internal structure – the way the story is told. As far as internal structure is concerned, the Ossian texts fit the pattern.

As a rule, ballad narratives begin precipitously, with little or no introductory setting. In the first stanza of "Der Sänger" (D149), for example, a king hears strange music coming from outside the palace gate and commands his page to let the singer in. Dialogue opens the story:

> "Was hör' ich draußen vor dem Tor,
> Was auf der Brücke schallen?
> Laß den Gesang vor unserm Ohr
> Im Saale widerhallen!"
> Der König sprach's, der Page lief,
> Der Page kam, der König rief:
> "Laßt mir herein den Alten!"

Other dramatic ballads that begin with dialogue include "Der Taucher" (D77), "Don Gayseros I" (D93/1), "Ritter Toggenburg" (D397), and "Uraniens Flucht" (D554). In each case, the narrator jumps into the action of his story, taking no time for descriptive detail. In ballads, such as "Die Nonne" (D208, 212), where the opening stanzas establish the physical setting for the action or create a context for the events of the story, the description is nevertheless brief and to the point:

> Es liebt' in Welschland irgendwo
> Ein schöner junger Ritter
> Ein Mädchen, das der Welt enfloh,
> Troz Klostertor und Gitter;
> Sprach viel von seiner Liebespein,
> Und schwur, auf seinen Knieen,
> Sie aus dem Kerker zu befreien,
> Und stets für sie zu glühen.

However they begin, ballads invariably move swiftly towards their climax, and then end abruptly. Rarely do the narratives involve any backtracking, incidental description, digression, or moralizing.[8] A single line of action extends from start to finish. No subsidiary plots deflect attention from the principal events of the story.

The subject matter of the dramatic ballads is also remarkably consistent. The narratives depict a person, or small group of persons, at some crucial moment in their lives. Usually the subjects possess a strange or remote quality. Particularly common are tales involving stock characters from medieval lore: maidens-in-distress, knights, kings, queens, nuns, and minstrels. The plots are conventional, the characters undeveloped as personalities. Another important (and overlapping) source is the realm of gothic mystery, with its ghastly apparitions, evil agents, and grisly murders (see the list below). During the mid 1810s, Schubert was evidently caught up in the contemporary fascination with the Middle Ages and taste for the macabre.

Principal subjects of Schubert's dramatic ballads

(a) *Medieval lore*
Der Taucher (D77)
Don Gayseros (D93/1–3)
Romanze (D114)
Ballade (D134)
Romanze, frag. (D144)
Der Sänger (D149)
Die Nonne (D208, 212)
Der Liedler (D209)
Adelwold und Emma (D211)
Die Bürgschaft (D246)
Ritter Toggenburg (D397)
Liedesend (D473)

(b) *Gothic mystery*
Leichenfantasie (D7)
Der Vatermörder (D10)
Erlkönig (D328)
Der Zwerg (D771)

Only a couple of Schubert's dramatic ballad texts involve characters from classical antiquity: "Amphiaraos" (D166) and "Uraniens Flucht" (D554). Perhaps because of their long-standing operatic associations, subjects derived from Greek mythology are generally presented in a straightforward dramatic mode, and set as dramatic scenes. Subjects involving medieval characters and customs, on the other hand, are invariably presented in a narrative mode. The correlation between medieval subjects and narrative verse likely stems from the prominent role during the Middle Ages of the wandering minstrel, who amused his audience with tales of love, treachery, and intrigue. Several of Schubert's dramatic ballads explicitly involve medieval minstrels ("Der Liedler,"

"Liedesend," "Der Sänger"). Nearly all of them have narrators who may be understood to play this role.

Finally, ballad texts are recognizable by their mood. Most ballads create a feeling of excitement and suspense, which intensifies right up to the climax of the story. At the conclusion, the reader/listener is left with a feeling of awe, revulsion, or horror. An extreme example is "Die Nonne" (D208, 212), the grisly tale of a nun who, having broken her vows of chastity, exacts revenge on her faithless seducer. She orders a band of assassins to murder him, then takes out his heart and tramples it to pieces. The ending is certain to make any listener squeamish:

> Die tiefen, hohlen Augen sprühn
> Ein düsterrotes Feuer,
> Und glühn, wie Schwefelflammen glühn,
> Durch ihren weißen Schleier.
> Sie gafft auf das zerrißne Herz,
> Mit wilder Rachgebärde,
> Und hebt es dreimal himmelwärts,
> Und wirft es auf die Erde;
>
> Und rollt die Augen voller Wut,
> Die eine Hölle blicken
> Und schüttelt aus dem Schleier Blut,
> Und stampft das Herz in Stücken.
> Ein bleicher Totenflimmer macht
> Indeß die Fenster helle.
> Der Wächter, der das Dorf bewacht,
> Sah's oft in der Kapelle.

Despite occasional lighter moments that provide relief from the mounting tension (e.g., the gentle supplication of the king's daughter in "Der Taucher"), ballad texts are never consciously humorous. The melodramatic plots and gruesome imagery may induce a smile from twentieth-century audiences unaccustomed to Romantic modes of thought, but laughter was not the poets' intention. On the contrary, the mood is one of grim intensity.

Simulation of drama

As we have observed, Schubert's dramatic ballad settings are characterized by many of the same musical traits as his dramatic scenes. Schubert brings the narratives "to life" by composing settings in a dramatic vein. The listener is led to imagine that he witnesses the events of the story in person, as if beholding a scene from an opera. Since the musical traits of dramatic scenes have already been examined at length, the present discussion will be brief.

Like dramatic scenes, dramatic ballads make ample use of recitative and arioso. In "Amphiaraos" (D166), the music alternates between passages headed "Recitativo" and others with a tempo marking. Most of the recitative passages have only a sparse chordal accompaniment. At frequent intervals, the recitative gives way to passages with repeated rhythmic patterns and/or a regular phrase structure. Often there is no clear textual reason for the change of style. In the first two stanzas, which maintain a consistent mood and contain no dialogue, the musical style changes eight times.

Alternation of contrasting musical styles is typical of Schubert's dramatic ballads. Sometimes separated by fermatas or rests, the different sections are further distinguished by changes of tempo, key, meter, texture, rhythm, phrasing, declamation, and accompanimental figuration. The sections may be long or short. The recitative may be secco or accompanied. The contrasting sections may be lyrical, martial, or even Lied-like, as in "Romanze" (D114) and "Ballade" (D134). The one constant is the idea of change.

Altering the musical style has a variety of possible functions. It might introduce a new character, call attention to a dramatic event, highlight a shift from narrative comment to dialogue, or reflect a change of mood. Alternatively, it might simply help prevent monotony and maintain the story's momentum.

Another characteristic that dramatic ballads share with dramatic scenes is throughcomposed form. As we have noted, throughcomposition permits each phase of the story to be reflected in the music, thus heightening the impression of an unfolding drama. In dramatic ballads, musical repetition is generally avoided because it creates a feeling of stasis that conflicts with the narrative's mounting suspense. To be sure, there are exceptions. "Ritter Toggenburg" (D397) and "Die Nonne" (D208, 212) both include strophic repetition. "Romanze" (D114) reverts to the opening music at the end, creating an impression of musical roundedness. In each case, the shift away from throughcomposition mirrors a shift in narrative perspective or tone. Nevertheless, throughcomposition remains the primary structural principle.

Progressive tonal structures, in which the music passes through many unrelated (or only loosely related) keys and concludes in a key different from that of the beginning, support the dramatic illusion. The frequent change of key in "Der Liedler" (D209) is typical. The first two stanzas, in which the minstrel tells his beloved that he must depart, are composed in the key of a minor. In the next three stanzas, which relate his journey through foreign lands, the tonal center moves through E♭ major, A♭ major, c♯ minor, B major, and D major. The rapid modulations continue throughout the song, finally concluding in A♭ major. Sometimes prepared, sometimes abrupt, the modulations illustrate particular aspects of the story (e.g., the minstrel's distant travels), and also convey the direction and pace of the action.

Lastly, Schubert attempts to simulate drama in his dramatic ballads by text-painting. In "Ballade" (D134), the furious battle between the hero and his enemy rages in angry dotted rhythms. In "Die Bürgschaft" (D246), the torrential downpour which threatens to impede the protagonist's journey is translated into a heavy onslaught of sixteenth notes. The energetic leaps of the youth in "Leichenfantasie" (D7) are expressed musically by ascending leaps of a sixth in the piano accompaniment. Text-painting of a slightly different sort occurs in "Der Sänger" (D149). Here, the thing translated into music is music itself. Schubert captures the sound of the minstrel's singing in the archaic musical style of the accompanimental introduction and interlude. Many more examples could be cited. In every case, text-painting intensifies the dramatic effect.

Narrative control

While all dramatic ballads exhibit dramatic musical traits, some also display distinctly non-dramatic features, such as strophic repetition, rounded forms, or tonal unity. These deviations from dramatic compositional models have much to do with the narrator's presence. After all, the ballad is not pure drama, but a combination of drama and narrative. Although downplayed, the narrator's role is not negligible.

A shift in narrative perspective or tone may give rise to musical repetition in an otherwise throughcomposed setting. The use of strophic form for the last three stanzas of "Die Nonne" (D208, 212), for example, was apparently inspired by the narrator's switch from past to present tense. Coming immediately after the narrative climax in stanza 8, the final three stanzas serve as a kind of epilogue, linking the gruesome events of the story to the present-day world of the listener. By forsaking throughcomposition, Schubert lets us know that the action of the story, if not its lurid imagery, is over.

Richard Capell has suggested that the strophic repetitions in stanzas 6–9 of "Ritter Toggenburg" (D397) bespeak compositional fatigue or laziness on Schubert's part, as well as on Zumsteeg's, whose setting served as Schubert's model.[9] There is a more likely explanation. In the story, a knight returns from battle to his loved one's castle, only to discover that she has just taken vows as a nun. Grief-stricken, the knight abandons his former life of heroism and glory, and becomes a hermit. At this point in the narrative, Schubert abandons throughcomposition in favor of strophic form. The musical repetitions help convey the lyrical suspension of time that the hermit experiences as he gazes from his hut for years on end at the convent window. A change in musical structure thus corresponds to a change in poetic tone: suspense gives way to serenity.

Narrators manipulate their subjects in other ways as well. They may retell certain events, or omit them entirely. Both of these strategies occur in "Der Taucher," resulting in musical repetition and breaks in musical continuity. Flashbacks, as in "Leichenfantasie" (D7), and foreshadowings, as in "Der Vatermörder" (D10), are also possible. These narrative techniques often involve text-painting and are particularly conducive to episodic musical forms.

In addition, narrators may alter the relation between story time (the amount of time encompassed by the action of the story) and narrative time (the amount of time it takes to tell the story). In dramatic ballads, story time usually far exceeds narrative time. A series of events extending through days, weeks, and even years, is related in a song lasting a period of minutes. (In lyrical genres, such as the strophic Lied and operatic aria, the length of the song usually exceeds the ostensible duration of the poetic subject. A passing emotion or sentiment expands to fill an entire song. In dramatic scenes, subject and song are of approximately equal duration.) At certain times during a ballad, however, the narrative pace may slow down, making the narration more "dramatic." This happens with the long accompanimental interlude at the end of "Der Taucher." A similar passage occurs in "Die Bürgschaft" (D246), during the middle of the fifth stanza. The accompanimental interlude helps convey the period of time that elapses between the friend's self-sacrifice and the sister's wedding.[10]

Complete story

Unlike dramatic scenes, ballads involve "complete" subjects – stories with a definite beginning, middle, and end. Because they relate a series of events, not just a single episode, they are often of enormous scope. Ranging from five to thirty pages, the dramatic ballads are among Schubert's longest songs, demanding of the listener greater endurance and attention to detail than most other Lieder.

Ex. 28 Schubert, "Amphiaraos" (D166), mm. 1–5

Dramatic ballads generally begin with a brief piano introduction that sets the mood.[11] In "Amphiaraos" (D166), powerful chords in dotted rhythms followed by sforzando octaves establish the heroic atmosphere of the opening battle scene (Ex. 28). In "Der Zwerg" (D771), the pulsing rhythmic motive and descending chromaticism in the piano's left hand, along with the minor mode and right hand tremolos, create an aura of evil and mystery (Ex. 29). The thundering triplet octaves that drive toward the dominant harmony in the introduction to "Erlkönig" (D328) are charged with excitement and suspense (Ex. 30).

Ex. 29 Schubert, "Der Zwerg" (D771), mm. 1–6

When the narrative begins *in medias res*, the voice's opening music is often unstable – modulating abruptly, changing styles, refusing to settle into a regular phrase structure. With several dramatic ballads, however, the opening music creates a frame for the events of the story through use of the "Romanzenton": the continuous quarter–eighth–quarter–eighth rhythmic pattern in $\frac{6}{8}$ meter that pervades both vocal line and accompaniment. We encounter this traditional pastoral style in the beginnings of "Romanze" (D114), "Ballade" (D134), and "Der Jüngling auf dem Hügel" (D702). Like a "Once upon a time. . ." story-book opening, the Romanzenton has a distancing effect, momentarily drawing attention to the role of the narrator before the action of the tale takes center stage.

In "Romanze" (D114), the Romanzenton music from the beginning of the song returns at the end, strengthening the impression of a narrative frame. (Schubert uses the Romanzenton style in the strophic repetitions at the end of "Die Nonne" [D208, 212], but not at the beginning.) Both the repetition of music and the use of the Romanzenton put an end to the narrative's forward drive. The events of the story, which the dramatic musical setting has brought to life, recede once more into the past. Schubert reminds the listener that the action just witnessed is but a tale.

Poetic and musical traits of the dramatic ballad

Ex. 30 Schubert, "Erlkönig" (D328), mm. 1–8

   Dramatic ballads always conclude with a solid cadence, giving a stamp of finality to the narrative outcome. Some songs display closed tonal structures, even when there have been many modulations to unrelated keys throughout. Returning to the opening key, like repeating the opening music, suggests an attempt to round the story into a satisfying whole.

The subject of narrative in music is extraordinarily complex. This chapter attempts no more than to survey some of the most salient characteristics of Schubert's dramatic ballads. The narrative techniques which these songs employ are also used in many of Schubert's mixed-genre Lieder. We now turn our attention to this important body of works.

PART III

Mixed-genre Lieder

Introduction to Part III

Many of Schubert's dramatic songs do not fit the general description of dramatic scenes or dramatic ballads. These more complex Lieder combine characteristic traits of the dramatic scene or ballad with those of lyrical genres, such as the lullaby, barcarolle, or lament.

Written primarily in the 1820s (but some dating back as early as 1814), the works which make up this third category of dramatic song may best be described as "mixed-genre Lieder" because they unite different vocal traditions. Their link to traditional Lieder is not simply the scoring for solo voice and piano (as in the dramatic scene and dramatic ballad) but also such traits as strophic form, melodic simplicity, subordinate accompaniment, closed tonality, unity of mood, and regular phrasing. The influence of dramatic vocal genres is manifest in throughcomposed forms, declamatory vocal lines, text-painting, open tonality, contrasting moods, and irregular phrasing.

Schubert's numerous mixed-genre Lieder differ from one another in the nature and proportions of their lyrical and dramatic qualities. It is helpful to imagine a spectrum of song types, with lyrical genres, such as the traditional strophic lullaby and lament, at one end and dramatic genres, such as the dramatic scene and dramatic ballad, at the other. Mindful of the dangers of oversimplification, we may gain insight into individual mixed-genre Lieder by attempting to place them on the spectrum. Some songs have a close affinity with traditional lyrical genres, but exhibit certain dramatic traits. These songs may be located near the traditional Lied end of the spectrum. Near the other end lie dramatic songs – monologues, dialogues, and ballads – with certain lyrical traits. In the middle are songs that combine lyrical and dramatic characteristics in roughly equal proportions.

The following chapters survey some of the most important compositional strategies Schubert employed in his mixed-genre Lieder. Discussion centers on the three categories described above: lyrical songs with admixtures of dramatic traits, dramatic songs with admixtures of lyrical traits, and lyrico-dramatic songs. Close analyses of songs belonging to each group lead to a clearer understanding of Schubert's compositional tactics when confronted with complex poetic texts.

7

Lyrical songs with admixtures of dramatic traits

Most of Schubert's mixed-genre Lieder are lyrical songs with admixtures of dramatic traits. We recognize these songs as essentially lyrical through their poetic subject, musical form, and characteristic gestures. Usually the song may be identified as belonging to (or a derivative of) a traditional song type: Grablied, Liebeslied, Ständchen, Frühlingslied, Barcarolle, etc. The type of poetic persona provides a strong clue to the generic origins of the song, as often does the title. Other factors, such as rhythm, meter, accompanimental pattern, and mode, also play an important role. While the song possesses certain dramatic musical traits, these do not hinder recognition of the particular Lied tradition from which the work emerged.

Early examples of this kind of mixed-genre Lied include many of the Matthisson songs from 1815, such as "Erinnerungen" (D98), "Der Abend" (D108), and "Lied der Liebe" (D109), in which short passages of recitative are incorporated into strophic settings. The temporary introduction of a declamatory vocal style supplies a heightened sense of dramatic immediacy to the words of the poetic persona. Frequently the use of recitative seems unmotivated by any particular event in the text, e.g., a change of tense, speaker, subject, or meter. Rather, it stems from Schubert's desire to intensify the emotional expression of the poem and to vivify the imagined scene.

Many "modified strophic" songs also belong to this category.[1] In modified strophic form, which appears in countless varieties in Schubert's Lieder, the first musical strophe does not repeat for every stanza of the poem but rather is replaced in one or more stanzas by varied or entirely new musical material. The static, lyrical effect of strophic repetition, associated with authentic and imitation folksongs, is disrupted by a dynamic impulse that produces certain musical modifications. Strophic variations are often used to illustrate "psychological action" in the text: a lover, fisherman, mother, or other traditional Lied persona experiences some sort of psychological change.

While Schubert began to compose modified strophic Lieder as early as 1812 with the first setting of Schiller's "Der Jüngling am Bache" (D30), he became particularly fond of this song type around 1816. A large percentage of the songs composed during the 1820s, including those in the three cycles, involve modified strophic repetition. An excellent example is "Das Wirtshaus"

(D911/21) from *Winterreise*. The musical form of this metaphorical Wanderlied – A A B A' – reflects the psychological development of the poetic speaker. The change of mood at the beginning of the third stanza, where the speaker realizes that he can find no resting place in death, is conveyed through new music. The fourth stanza, in which he continues sadly on his life journey, returns to the opening music, now recast in the minor mode. Schubert's altered form of the "A" material suggests that while the speaker's predicament remains the same, he has acquired a new understanding of his fate.[2]

Other lyrical songs introduce dramatic elements in different ways, and for different reasons. "Bertas Lied in der Nacht" (D653), a lullaby, is through-composed and begins and ends in different keys. "Totengräbers Heimweh" (D842) starts as a conventional work song and concludes as a dramatic monologue. The several versions of Mignon's lament "Nur wer die Sehnsucht kennt" (D310, 359, 481, 877/1, 877/4) introduce melodramatic tremolos midway through the song, at the phrase "Es schwindelt mir."

"Gretchen am Spinnrade" (D118) initially appears to be a traditional spinning song. Half-way through, however, the poetic persona stops singing, drawing the listener's attention to the dramatic context for the Lied – Gretchen's sorrowful plight. In one important respect the song is like a dramatic scene: the words belong to an identifiable character and are embedded in a particular dramatic context.[3] By contrast, the words of a traditional Lied belong to a character *type* (e.g., a particular lullaby may be sung by any mother). The fact that strophic form is only hinted at (through the refrain "Meine Ruh ist hin"), rather than actually present, supports the claim that "Gretchen am Spinnrade" is not a traditional spinning song, like "Die Spinnerin" (D247), but a mixed-genre Lied.

A representative selection of mixed-genre Lieder that may be described as lyrical songs with admixtures of dramatic traits is listed below.[4]

Lyrical songs with admixtures of dramatic traits

D98	Erinnerungen
D108	Der Abend
D109	Lied der Liebe
D118	Gretchen am Spinnrade
D121	Schäfers Klagelied
D197	An die Apfelbäume wo ich Julien erblickte
D217	Kolmas Klage
D298	Liane
D361	Am Bach im Frühling
D413	Entzückung
D495	Abendlied der Fürstin
D516	Sehnsucht
D550	Die Forelle
D553	Auf der Donau
D585	Atys

D588	Der Alpenjäger
D614	An den Mond in einer Herbstnacht
D653	Bertas Lied in der Nacht
D672	Nachtstücke
D712	Die gefangenen Sänger
D731	Der Blumen Schmerz
D795/4	Danksagung an den Bach
D795/5	Am Feierabend
D795/6	Der Neugierige
D795/10	Tränenregen
D805	Der Sieg
D808	Gondelfahrer
D842	Totengräbers Heimweh
D851	Das Heimweh
D877/4	Nur wer die Sehnsucht kennt
D879	Sehnsucht
D880	Im Freien
D882	Im Frühling
D911/1	Gute Nacht
D911/5	Der Lindenbaum
D911/7	Auf dem Flusse
D911/11	Frühlingstraum
D911/12	Einsamkeit
D911/16	Letzte Hoffnung
D911/20	Der Wegweiser
D911/21	Das Wirtshaus
D932	Der Kreuzzug
D957/9	Ihr Bild

Schubert's compositional strategies in these and other lyrical songs with admixtures of dramatic traits are manifold. A full survey of such Lieder is beyond the scope of this study. Nevertheless, we can acquire a better understanding of works at the lyrical end of the song spectrum through a detailed analysis of one particularly fine example.

"Schäfers Klagelied" (D121)

On February 28, 1819, a small gathering of Viennese society witnessed the first public performance of a Schubert song. Third on Edward Jaell's eclectic program of musical works and poetic recitations was the young composer's "Schäfers Klagelied" (D121), a Goethe setting dating from 1814.[5] Sung by the well-known tenor Franz Jäger, an opera singer at the Theater an der Wien, the little shepherd's lament met with great enthusiasm. Several papers, including the Vienna *Theaterzeitung*, the Berlin *Gesellschafter*, and the Leipzig *Allgemeine musikalische Zeitung*, lavished praise on both the song and Schubert's compositional talent.[6]

Three years later (shortly after the song's publication by Cappi & Diabelli as Op. 3, no. 1), a more extensive critique of "Schäfers Klagelied" appeared. Friederich von Hentl described the song in glowing terms:[7]

Here everything combines to make a perfect musical work. The peculiar pastoral tone is admirably suggested; it is expressed first of all by the melody. The accompaniment is suitable and holds together the melodies differentiated by the characteristic changes. These melodies are delightful in themselves and serve as aesthetic ideas even without the words and harmony. Each note must remain unchanged if the melody is not to be ruined – a sure sign of its organic nature! The characterization is so incisive that it requires no analysis in order to be generally felt. The transitions between one characteristic expression and another are also most natural and affecting here.

Hentl's remarks betray the Romantic sensibility of his time. While outdated, his preoccupation with artistic organicism raises important questions about Schubert's setting. What kinds of characteristic expression are involved in the song, and what aesthetic purpose is served by the modulation from one to another? How does the song strike a balance between multiplicity of expression and unity of form? For what poetic end does Schubert strive to create an "organic" musical structure? These questions are all pertinent to an interpretation of Schubert's setting. For while initially posing as a simple folk song, "Schäfers Klagelied" reveals a degree of artistry in both poetry and music uncharacteristic of the oral tradition.

The sectional musical structure which Hentl praises closely follows the stanzaic outlines of Goethe's text (translation on pp. 145–146). With one exception, each of the six poetic stanzas is presented as a cohesive musical unit. Stanza 4, breaking the principle of one-to-one correspondence, divides into two subsections. A letter diagram helps clarify the relationship between the poetic and musical structures.[8]

A	Da droben auf jenem Berge,
	Da steh' ich tausendmal,
	An meinem Stabe hingebogen,
	Und schaue hinab in das Thal.
B	Dann folg' ich der weidenden Heerde,
	Mein Hündchen bewahret mir sie;
	Ich bin herunter gekommen
	Und weiß doch selber nicht wie.
C	Da stehet von schönen Blumen,
	Da steht die ganze Wiese so voll;
	Ich breche sie, ohne zu wissen,
	Wem ich sie geben soll.
D1	Und Regen, Sturm und Gewitter
	Verpass' ich unter dem Baum.
D2	Die Thüre dort bleibet verschlossen;
	Doch alles ist leider ein Traum.

B'   Es stehet ein Regenbogen
Wohl über jenem Haus,
Sie aber ist fortgezogen,
Und weit in das Land hinaus.

A'   Hinaus in das Land und weiter,
Vielleicht gar über die See.
Vorüber, ihr Schafe, nur vorüber!
Dem Schäfer ist gar so weh.
Vorüber, ihr Schafe, nur vorüber!
Dem Schäfer ist gar so weh.

Schubert's musical structure, with its sharply differentiated sections, is unusual on several counts. The title of the song (both Goethe's and Schubert's) suggests that the work belongs to a traditional musical genre – the Klagelied, or lament. Like most types of Volkslieder, the Klagelied generally has a strophic form, with each poetic stanza sung to the same musical strophe. The musical repetition helps to express the text's single poetic sentiment: the sorrow of loss. Schubert himself composed several strophic Klagelieder, including Rochlitz's "Klaglied" (D23), Schiller's "Des Mädchens Klage" (D191), Hölty's "Die Laube" (D214), and Fouqué's "Lied" (D373). Since the text of "Schäfers Klagelied" contains no structural irregularities preventing strophic repetition, one expects a purely strophic setting. Schubert frustrates these expectations.

The musical structure of "Schäfers Klagelied" involves a mixture of throughcomposition and repetition. While the first four stanzas are each set to new music, the last two stanzas repeat earlier sections. Particularly unusual is the setting of stanzas 5 and 6, which, by repeating the music of stanzas 1 and 2 in reverse order, creates a nearly symmetrical large-scale form: A B C D B' A'. A similar, but far more conventional, sectional structure outlines a large tri-partite form: A B C D A' B'. As we shall see, Schubert's unconventional reprise is better suited to the inner dynamics of the poetry.

Goethe's text, interestingly enough, originated as a parody of an actual folk song. According to an undated letter by F. K. J. Schütz, a professor at the University of Jena and an acquaintance of the poet's, Goethe was inspired by a Rhenish folksong he heard performed at a party.[9] The words to the song were reportedly of little poetic value, but the music was quite pleasing and made a strong impression on Goethe. He decided to write new words to be sung to the existing melody, and by the following day had produced "Da droben auf jenem Berge." Schütz adds that Goethe planned to enrich other folk melodies with new words in a similar manner. The party to which Schütz refers must have occurred in late 1801 or early 1802, for on February 22, 1802, Caroline Schlegel sent her husband August Wilhelm a copy of "Schäfers Klagelied," along with a note describing it as "a little romance which Goethe made after a folk melody that he recently heard here and that comes from the Rhine."[10]

Several sources preserve variants of the Rhenish folk song which captured Goethe's fancy. Both folk text and melody appear in a short article entitled "Volklieder" in Johann Friedrich Reichardt's *Musikalisches Kunstmagazin* of 1782 (Ex. 31) (translation on pp. 146–147).[11] In his short commentary, Reichardt states that, as so often happens, the melody of this folk song antedates the words. Claiming that the tune was originally "ein Jägerhornstück," Reichardt takes the liberty of writing beneath it his own accompaniment – "a second voice in the manner of a hunting horn."[12] With the horn fifths of Reichardt's accompaniment, the music clearly takes on the character of a hunting song. But even alone, the tune's sprightly rhythms (written in $\frac{3}{8}$, notwithstanding the notated $\frac{3}{4}$ time signature) and major mode seem more appropriate for expressing the joys of the hunt than the sorrow of lovers parting. Reichardt was probably correct that the words were a later addition. The uneasy partnership of musical mood and poetic sentiment, as well as the textual disjunction between stanzas 3 and 4 (suggesting the text was compiled sequentially), supports this claim.

Ex. 31 Reichardt, "Dort droben in jenem Thale." From Reichardt, ed.,
Musikalisches Kunstmagazin (Berlin, 1782), vol. I, p. 99

Mixed-genre Lieder

Dort droben in jenem Thale
Da treibet das Wasser das Rad;
Es treibet nichts anders als Liebe
Vom Abend bis an den Tag.

Das Mühlrad ist zersprungen
Die Lieb hat noch kein End,
Wenn zwey von einander scheiden
So geben sich einander die Händ.

Ach! Scheiden, ach Scheiden
Wer hat Scheiden erdacht,
Es hat mein jung frisch Leben
Zum Untergange gebracht.

Es ist ja kein Apfel so schön so rund
Es stecken zwey Kernlein drin'n
Es ist kein Mädchen im Lande
Es hat ein'n falschen Sinn.

Wer kann dann nun vertrauen?
Scheidt' er ihnen aus dem Aug:
Ein falscher Sinn, ein hoher Muth
Ist aller Jungfern ihr Brauch.

Dort in meines Vaters Lustgarten
Da stehen zwey Bäumelein
Das eine das träget Muskaten,
Das andre braun Nägelein.

Muskaten die sind süße,
Braun Nägelein riechen gar wohl
Die will ich mein'n Schätzgen verehren
Daß es dran riechen soll.

Des Knaben Wunderhorn, Arnim and Brentano's famous Lieder collection of 1806–08, contains a version of the text, entitled "Müllers Abschied," which corresponds to the first three stanzas of Reichardt's folk song.[13]

Müllers Abschied (translation on p. 147)

Da droben auf jenem Berge
Da steht ein goldnes Haus,
Da schauen wohl alle Frühmorgen
Drei schöne Jungfrauen heraus.

Die eine, die heißet Elisabeth,
Die andre Bernharda mein,
Die dritte, die will ich nicht nennen,
Die sollt mein eigen sein.

Da unten in jenem Tale
Da treibt das Wasser ein Rad,
Das treibet nichts als Liebe
Vom Abend bis wieder an Tag;

Das Rad, das ist gebrochen,
Die Liebe, die hat ein End,
Und wenn zwei Liebende scheiden
Sie reichen einander die Händ.

Ach Scheiden, ach, ach!
Wer hat doch das Scheiden erdacht,
Das hat mein jung frisch Herzelein
So frühzeitig traurig gemacht.

Dies Liedlein, ach, ach!
Hat wohl ein Müller erdacht,
Den hat des Ritters Töchterlein
Vom Lieben zum Scheiden gebracht.

Assuming that the tunes were widely known (or perhaps lacking any efficient means to transcribe them), Arnim and Brentano printed only the Lieder texts. But this music need not be considered wholly lost, for other sources contain what must be close variants. Erk and Böhme's *Deutscher Liederhort* of 1893–94, for example, includes a folk song with nearly the identical text (Ex. 32).[14] Aside from its slightly shorter length and a few details, the Erk–Böhme variant shows no significant differences from the *Wunderhorn* variant. Interestingly, the Erk–Böhme folk song bears a marked similarity in melodic contour and rhythm to Reichardt's "hunting" tune. One may surmise that the Erk–Böhme variant represents a close approximation of the folk song which fired Goethe's imagination.

Ex. 32 "Das Mühlrad." From *Deutscher Liederhort*, ed. Ludwig Erk and Franz
M. Böhme (3 vols., Leipzig, 1893–94), vol. II, pp. 234–235

Da droben auf jenem Berge
Da steht ein hohes Haus,
Da schauen wol alle Frühmorgen
Drei schöne Jungfrauen heraus.

Die eine heißt Susanne
Die andere Anne-Marei;
Die dritte die darf ich nicht nennen
Weil sie es mein eigen soll sein.

Da drunten in jenen Thale
Da treibet das Wasser ein Rad
Das mahlet nichts als Liebe
Vom Morgen bis Abend spät.

Das Mühlrad ist zerbrochen,
Die Liebe hat noch kein End –
Und wenn sich zwei Herzliebchen scheiden,
So reichen's einander die Händ.

Ach Scheiden, du bitteres Scheiden!
Wer hat doch das Scheiden erdacht?
Der hat ja mein jung frisch Herze
Aus Freuden in Trauren gebracht.

Although "Schäfers Klagelied" was in private circulation as early as 1802,[15] Goethe did not actually publish the poem until 1804. During this year, two different editions of Goethe's folk song parodies appeared on the market.[16] The first edition, *Taschenbuch aufs Jahr 1804*, contains a selection of poems which, like "Schäfers Klagelied," were inspired by folk song. While this edition, like the *Wunderhorn* collection, contains only texts, the musical origin of the poetry is documented in a letter that Schiller sent to the publisher (Cotta) in May 1802:[17] According to Schiller, Goethe wanted to edit a collection of poems which he had written to be sung to well-known melodies. Schiller vouches for the excellence of Goethe's verses, stating that they not only elevate the melodies but in fact fit them better than the original song texts.

The second edition of Goethe's folk song parodies was specifically intended for musicians. Edited and arranged (under Goethe's supervision) by Wilhelm Ehlers, the *Gesänge mit Begleitung der Chitarre* includes a musical setting of "Schäfers Klagelied" whose melody is similar to, but not identical with, both of the folk song variants discussed above (Ex. 33). The melodic shape of the opening and closing bars is closely related, but the middle section differs considerably. The extent to which Ehlers actually borrowed from the oral tradition remains unclear. While perhaps not a direct transcription of folk song, Ehlers's setting is nevertheless certainly a close imitation.

Goethe's text, on the other hand, is far more complex than actual folk song. Schütz and Schiller both speak of Goethe's parody technique as a type of poetic "enrichment" (*bereichern*), a way of combining traditional and modern

Lyrical songs with admixtures of dramatic traits

Ex. 33 Ehlers, "Schäfers Klagelied." From Frederick W. Sternfeld, *Goethe and Music: A List of Parodies and Goethe's Relationship to Music* (New York, 1954), p. 11

Da dro - ben auf je - nem Ber - ge da steh ich tau - send mal An___ mei - nem Sta - be ge - bo - gen Und schau - e hin - ab in das Tal.

elements. Goethe's poem thus should not be understood as an imitation folk text, duplicating in manner and spirit the folk poetry of his day. Instead, it represents an enrichment or modernization of folk poetry – a self-conscious re-creation of its bucolic style, a reenactment of its rustic themes. This point, we will see, is crucial for an understanding of Schubert's song.

A comparison of "Schäfers Klagelied" with "Müllers Abschied" (the *Wunderhorn* folk text) illustrates this complexity.[18] The two texts exhibit nearly identical formal characteristics. Both texts have four lines in each stanza and three stressed syllables in each line. They also have the same general rhyme scheme: abcb. These shared formal traits arise from the melodic shape of the folk tune with which both texts are associated, and they are largely responsible for the folk song character of Goethe's text.

The formal similarities between the two texts, however, are overshadowed by substantive contrasts. While both texts involve basically the same subject – the mourning of lost love – their personae are markedly different. In the Wunderhorn text, the singer woefully admits that he is a miller "den hat des Ritters Töchterlein / Vom Lieben zum Scheiden gebracht." Although he never gives his lover's name (presumably too painful a task for this heart-broken lad), there is nothing mysterious about her identity. She, like her sisters Elisabeth and Bernharda, is the knight's daughter and lives in a golden castle "da droben auf jenem Berge." Nor is there much doubt about the source of the miller's misery. Too great a distance separates the mill stream in the valley from the castle on the mountain, and the singer from his mistress. The lowly miller is not worthy of the knight's daughter.

In Goethe's poem, a shepherd, rather than a miller, laments the loss of his loved one. Here, oddly enough, the girl's identity remains wholly obscure. We learn nothing about her aside from the fact that she has gone away, "Hinaus in das Land und weiter/Vielleicht gar über die See." Even more perplexing, the shepherd does not actually mention her until halfway through the fifth stanza. Not until the last two lines of the poem ("Vorüber, ihr Schafe, vorüber / Dem Schäfer ist gar so weh,") does one sense the full force of his grief. Up until this point, one might not even recognize the poem as a lament, so disguised are the shepherd's emotions, so veiled are his thoughts. When the shepherd speaks the third stanza ("Da stehet von schönen Blumen / Die ganze Wiese so voll / Ich breche sie ohne zu wissen / Wem ich sie geben soll,"), one does not suspect a hidden reference to his departed love, for he has not yet revealed his sorrow. Even when, after the thunderstorm, he finds that "Die Thüre dort bleibet verschlossen," one remains unaware of the significance of this discovery. Unlike that of the miller, the shepherd's predicament is shrouded in mystery.

It seems not insignificant that Goethe has transformed the *Wunderhorn* miller into a shepherd. Roaming the hills and valleys with his flock of sheep, Goethe's shepherd bears a striking resemblance to the Romantic wanderer, a ubiquitous figure in early nineteenth-century poetry. This is not to say that millers cannot or do not play the wanderer role; witness the protagonist of *Die schöne Müllerin*. Rather, the job of watching over one's sheep involves the activity of wandering which the task of grinding grain at a mill does not. Goethe takes advantage of this difference.

Like the Romantic wanderer, Goethe's shepherd seems to quest after something he will never attain. In this sense, he resembles the lonesome, dejected persona of Schmidt's "Der Wanderer" (D489, 493) who also vainly seeks happiness. Both figures wander down the mountainside and through the fields in search of their ideals; both ultimately come to the shattering realization that their hopes are nothing but dreams. Happiness will always elude them: "Dort wo du nicht bist, dort ist das Glück." Goethe's poem, to be sure, does not completely forsake the sentimental strain of the *Wunderhorn* verses. Like "Müllers Abschied," it draws both a smile and a tear. But here, sentimentality combines with seriousness. The pretty pastoral subject takes on a new profundity.

In depicting the plight of his romanticized shepherd, Goethe chooses a narrative mode of presentation; the shepherd tells the story of his wanderings. The shepherd's narrative stance differs fundamentally from the miller's lyrical reflection. In "Schäfers Klagelied," every stanza represents a different stage of the story, containing unique images and incidents. The succession of stanzas thus marks the passage of narrative time. The miller's lament, by contrast, focuses solely on the "present" moment of reflective sorrow. Yet, as with most autobiographical narratives, the shepherd's story comes close to actual drama. His imaginings take on the color of reality. In the first stanza, the shepherd points to the mountain where he habitually stands, looking down into the valley. At this moment, one pictures him standing on a neighboring hilltop. In the second stanza, images from the past begin to intrude on his imagination. It seems to him that he is once again in the valley, following his sheep: "Dann folg ich der weidenden Heerde, / Mein Hündchen bewahret mir sie; / Ich bin herunter gekommen / Und weiß doch selber nicht wie." Not until the fifth stanza does this imagery from the past begin to recede. Once again, he faces present reality.

Schubert's setting captures the complexities of Goethe's poem by drawing upon diverse musical traditions. The song immediately announces its close ties to folk music with the pastoral $\frac{6}{8}$ meter. Both of the "Da droben" folk song variants discussed above, as well as Ehlers's Goethe setting, have essentially this same meter.[19] In addition, Schubert begins the song with the traditional ballad rhythm of alternating quarters and eighths in the piano accompaniment and a slightly decorated version in the vocal part (Ex. 34). This pattern is particularly appropriate given the song's narrative mode. It suggests a link to other ballad or romance settings, such as Schiller's "Das Mädchen aus der Fremde" (D117) and Matthisson's "Romanze" (D114). Although the piano drops this characteristic rhythm after only a few bars, the association retains its force, for the voice never strays far from the basic pattern.

Ex. 34 Schubert, "Schäfers Klagelied" (D121), mm. 1–4

The music's folk song character also arises from its air of simplicity. The piano accompaniment starts with a bare chordal texture that provides light harmonic support for the vocal part. Even when the accompanimental figuration becomes more involved in the succeeding stanzas, the piano continues to play a primarily supportive role. As in folk song, it cannot be considered an equal partner with the voice.

The vocal part, too, steers clear of technical difficulties. No daring leaps, intense chromaticism, or ornate melismata are to be found in its modest, diatonic melody. It has the feel of a tune that anyone could sing. Interestingly, the repeated neighbor-note pattern at the beginning of the vocal part bears a strong resemblance to the opening neighbor-note motion of the folk song variants discussed above. This musical similarity parallels the similarity between the opening lines of Goethe's poem and the folk texts and suggests that Schubert, like Goethe, conceived his work as a parody.

But while "Schäfers Klagelied" clearly draws upon the tradition of folk song, especially the Klagelied and strophic ballad, it could never be mistaken for one. This song does not belong in the same class as Hölty's "Der Traum" (D213), Kosegarten's "Das Finden" (D219), or Schiller's "An den Frühling" (D283) – original works which might well pass for traditional Volkslieder. As early as the fourth measure, Schubert hints that his setting is not confined to the immediate realm of folk song by disrupting the prevailing metrical scheme with an early vocal entrance: mm. 4–8 are anticipated by half a measure. (Schubert accomplishes this disruption by adding the syllable "hin" to the word "gebogen" in line 3 of Goethe's text.)

In addition to folk song, Schubert's setting also borrows elements from dramatic vocal genres. Perhaps most obvious is its sectional structure, a characteristic of dramatic scenes and ballads. Each musical section depicts the imagery in the accompanying text. Thus, in setting the first stanza, Schubert paints the pastoral scene with a plaintive $\frac{6}{8}$ melody. The musical illustration, subtly expressed with an upward vocal leap at the word "Berge," becomes explicit with the long melodic descent at the poetic phrase "und schaue hinab in das Thal." Later, in the third stanza, the frolicsome piano figuration and bouncy vocal rhythm, reminiscent of Frühlingslieder, depict the shepherd's buoyant spirit as he wanders through the countryside. Immediately following, the piano suddenly begins a thunderous pounding of sixteenth-note chords – easily recognizable (especially from dramatic ballads and melodrama) as the musical equivalent of a storm (Ex. 35). As each image from the past intrudes upon the shepherd's imagination, the music begins a new section.

As in many of his dramatic scenes and ballads, Schubert uses modulation as a means of representing textual action. With each poetic stanza, the music shifts to a new key area (stanza 4, the one exception, centers on two key areas) (Ex. 36). Each change of harmonic focus signals a new development in the shepherd's story.

But the relation between this wide-ranging harmonic scheme and the poetic narrative runs much deeper. Schubert sets the first stanza as a balanced eight-measure period, beginning and ending in the tonic (C minor). The harmonic stability of this opening section mirrors the stationary subject: the shepherd imagines himself leaning against his staff, high up on the mountain. Hinting at the first bit of action, a short accompanimental transition modulates to the mediant (mm. 9–10). With this harmonic event, the past begins to intrude on the present.

The second stanza, significantly, is not set to a harmonically closed period. The shepherd now remembers how he used to follow his sheep. The mediant harmony, first stabilized by the drone-like pedal point, takes a last minute turn to the dominant minor (mm. 16–19). This startling modulation seems to be motivated by the shepherd's sudden uncertainty: "Ich bin herunter gekommen/Und weiß doch selber nicht wie." The darkened harmony captures the unexpected solemnity of his tone. But the modulation also reflects the distance (both physical and imaginative) he has traversed in his wanderings.

After another short piano transition (mm. 19–20), also modulating, the third stanza begins in the key of the submediant. Again, the change of harmonic focus suggests new action. Here, the shepherd imagines himself picking flowers in a meadow. The stable pedal point harmonies of mm. 21–24 create the impression that he is happy and carefree. But with the introduction of the Db major and minor harmonies of m. 25, his tone suddenly becomes wistful: "Ich breche sie, ohne zu wissen, / Wem ich sie geben soll." Measure 25 marks the first encroachment of non-diatonic harmonies. As the shepherd's inner turmoil mounts, the harmony veers farther and farther from the original tonic.

In stanza 4 – the moment of psychological and physical crisis – the harmony reaches its most distant point. The sudden unleashing of natural forces in the thunderstorm parallels and symbolizes the rush of emotions that the shepherd experiences at the thought of his loneliness. His anger lashes out in the remote key of ab minor (m. 27). When, in m. 31, the harmony shifts to the mediant (Cb major) of this key, one senses that the poor shepherd has reached the brink of despair. He has traveled a great distance from the psychological calm of the mountain top. The music comes to a complete stop in m. 33. The shepherd can proceed no further, and is at a loss for how to return.

In mm. 35–38, as the shepherd's fantasy of love and happiness begins to slip away ("Die Thüre bleibet verschlossen / Doch alles ist leider ein Traum"), the Cb major harmony slides down chromatically to Bb, or V/III. The path home is now clear. Stanza 5, set to the music of stanza 2, again centers around the mediant of the original key. The shepherd is retracing his steps. Still partially caught up in his dream world ("Es stehet ein Regenbogen / Wohl über jenem Haus"), he gradually comes to recognize the reality of his loss. For the first time in the song, he mentions the girl who has left him

Ex. 35 Schubert, "Schäfers Klagelied" (D121), mm. 20–33

110

Ex. 36 Harmonic structure of "Schäfers Klagelied" (D121)

Stanza:	1	2	3	4		5	6
Key:	c	E♭	A♭	a♭	C♭	E♭	c
	i	III	VI	vi	III/vi	III	i

("Sie aber ist fortgezogen, / Und weit in das Land hinaus").[20] As his hopes and dreams fade, the harmony circles back to the tonic.

The last stanza, repeating (in a slightly extended version) the music of the first, reveals the extent of the shepherd's sorrow: "Vorüber, ihr Schafe, vorüber! / Dem Schäfer ist gar so weh." Here, the stability of harmony has new meaning. Like the prototypical Romantic wanderer, the shepherd can never reach his goal; he will continue in his quest forever. The rounded harmonic structure of this final section suggests the permanence of his fate.

The quasi-dramatic narration of Goethe's text is also illustrated in Schubert's handling of rhythm. Especially remarkable are the rhythmic transformations of the piano accompaniment. The first stanza, with its stationary speaker, moves in slow note values: m. 1 establishes a pattern of alternating quarters and eighths, but most of the eight-measure period moves at an even slower pace.

The piano transition of mm. 9–10 introduces the eighth note motion which governs the entire second stanza. The increased rhythmic activity of this next section supports the dramatic illusion. Here, the shepherd imagines himself following his flock through the valley. The eighth note motion, contrasting with the slow accompaniment of the first stanza, depicts (although not literally) his walking pace.

The third stanza, continuing the trend toward greater rhythmic excitement, moves in sixteenth notes. No longer walking, the shepherd skips merrily through the fields, picking flowers as he goes. The rhythmic acceleration, however, also portrays his psychological agitation as he nears his beloved's house. The sixteenth note motion persists through the thunderstorm in the first half of the fourth stanza. Through a change of texture, the frolicsome accompanimental rhythm in mm. 21–27 suddenly becomes tempestuous

Ex. 37 Schubert, "Schäfers Klagelied" (D121), mm. 33–38

at m. 28. The pounding sixteenths capture the fury of both natural and psychological storms.

After the complete break of m. 33, the accompaniment reverts to the drawn-out pace of dotted quarter notes in five measures of quasi-recitative – an apt musical illustration of the calm after the storm (Ex. 37). The wind and rain are gone; the shepherd sadly recognizes all has been but a dream.

With the return of the second stanza's music in m. 39, and the return of the eighth note motion, the poet starts to head back in the direction from which he came. One imagines him slowly, resignedly, walking back up the mountain. With the return of the first stanza's music in m. 48, he arrives at his point of origin. His dream is over.

Ex. 38 Rhythmic reduction of the vocal line in "Schäfers Klagelied" (D121), stanzas 1–2

The rhythm of the vocal line, while far less variable than that of the accompaniment, supports these expressive transformations. Like the piano, the voice adopts a walking pace of even eighths beginning in line 5 (Ex. 38). Three of the four lines in stanza 2 begin with the even eighth note rhythm (even line 7, whose metrical pattern does not call for it), whereas none of the lines in stanza 1 does.

Occasionally, the rhythm of the vocal line alone creates an impression of dramatic immediacy. In the second stanza, for example, the shepherd stops abruptly after saying "Ich bin herunter gekommen"; a full measure of silence intervenes before he continues with the next line. The musical period is thus extended to an irregular nine measures (mm. 11–19). This dramatic pause has no place in a traditional folk song. Like a character on stage, the shepherd experiences *present* uncertainty as he stops to ponder how he has come so low ("Ich bin herunter gekommen/und weiß doch selber nicht wie").

A similar dramatic effect occurs in the last line of stanza 3, once again resulting from Schubert's manipulation of the vocal rhythm. The drastic lengthening of the word "geben" in m. 27, without precedent in the song, gives the music a taste of vocal grandeur.

Schubert's fusion of folk song and drama in "Schäfers Klagelied" ingeniously reflects the "pseudo-iterative" mode of Goethe's text. An iterative narrative describes events which are repetitive in nature. Folk ballads generally fall into this category. The poignant little tragedy of the wild rose in Goethe's "Heidenröslein" (D257), to take one well-known example, symbolizes the universal story of conquest and defeat. The rose's vain struggle with the youth represents the retelling of an old tale. Schubert's use of strophic form helps convey the repetitive nature of the plot. In "Schäfers Klagelied," the shepherd begins his narrative in an iterative manner by pointing to the mountain where he has stood "tausend mal." The ensuing description of his wandering course down its slope and through the valley thus seems to refer to a habitual activity, rather than a specific, one-time event. Quickly, however, one senses that the shepherd provides too much detail for a purely iterative narrative. It is unlikely that he picks flowers, sits out a thunderstorm, and tries the locked door of his lover's house every day. The abundance of detail suggests that the text works on a dramatic as well as narrative level: in telling his story, the shepherd experiences it as real. Schubert depicts this modal ambiguity by combining elements from folk and dramatic musical genres.

We are finally in a position to understand both the song's organic nature and its unusual structural arrangement. The A B C D B' A' sectional form is a clever compositional solution to the challenge of Goethe's pseudo-iterative text. Schubert creates a musical illustration of the shepherd's imaginative trek down into the valley and back again. The reversed order of the final two musical sections portrays both the shepherd's return to the mountain and his awakening to reality; he emerges from the depths of both the valley and his dream world. The initial impulse of throughcomposition, granting dramatic immediacy to his imagined journey, gives way to repetition as the music doubles back on itself. Multiplicity of expression balances with unity of form – a compositional strategy well suited to this sorrowful "psychological" drama.

8

Dramatic songs with admixtures of lyrical traits

Dramatic songs with admixtures of lyrical traits appear infrequently in Schubert's Lied oeuvre, but include some of his best works. Through their subject, presentational mode, musical style, and structure, these songs are recognizable as dramatic monologues, dialogues, or ballads, but they differ significantly from the simpler types of dramatic song. By incorporating traditional Lied traits, such as tonal and motivic unity, into what are essentially dramatic settings, Schubert produces powerful and artistically satisfying works. These songs "correct" some of the problems associated with the simpler dramatic scenes and dramatic ballads, which have often been criticized as long, rambling, and shapeless. The more complex mixed-genre dramatic songs have received almost universal praise.

In some mixed-genre songs, a brief lyrical section is enclosed within the dramatic setting. Such is the case with "Lied des Orpheus" (D474), a dramatic monologue delivered by the legendary singer at the entrance to Hades. At the end of the second stanza, Orpheus commands the creatures who block his passage: "Horchet auf mein Lied!" Stanzas 3–6 constitute the lyrical verses of this song-within-a-song. Here, in recalling the beauties of the world above, Orpheus appeals to the deepest sympathies of those who may once also have known the torment of love. The musical setting possesses a far more lyrical character than that of the preceding stanzas, when Orpheus was ostensibly speaking. Composed in $\frac{3}{4}$ rather than $\frac{4}{4}$ meter, Orpheus' "Lied" is characterized by balanced phrasing, melismatic writing, text repetition, poignant dissonances, and affective vocal leaps. The lilting triplet rhythms which pervade the evenly textured accompanimental part have a particularly "songful" effect. Although stanzas 3–6 are not set strophically, the musical character of this section is easily recognizable as that of the traditional Lied.

While both powerful and appealing, "Lied des Orpheus" ultimately fails to integrate its dramatic and lyrical aspects. An undeniably superior compositional approach is exemplified by Schubert's "Erlkönig" (D328). A dramatic ballad unlike any other, the setting builds dramatic suspense within a unified musical framework. As is typical of ballads, the song includes numerous modulations which help portray the various stages of the narrative. However, in the last stanza (which, like the first, is spoken by the narrator) the music returns to the opening key of g minor. The internal modulations are not haphazard, as in many of Schubert's ballads, but rather organized motivically around the tonal center of the piece. The pounding triplet rhythms which sound in the accompaniment through nearly the whole song – suggesting variously the motion of the galloping horse and the seductive, carousel-like atmosphere of the Erlking's world – add to the impression of musical unity. The same is true of the boy's refrain "Mein Vater, mein Vater" and the return of the piano's opening motive in the last stanza. These various unifying elements, traditionally associated with lyrical genres, enable the story to unfold within an aesthetically rounded structure. This roundedness gives a stamp of finality to the gruesome ending, intensifying the listener's shock.

A selection of mixed-genre Lieder that may be described as dramatic songs with admixtures of lyrical traits is given in the list below.

Dramatic songs with admixtures of lyrical traits

D301	Lambertine
D328	Erlkönig
D369	An Schwager Kronos
D450	Fragment aus dem Aeschylus
D474	Lied des Orpheus
D489, 493	Der Wanderer
D526	Fahrt zum Hades
D541	Memnon
D594	Der Kampf
D698	Liebeslauschen
D713	Der Unglückliche
D771	Der Zwerg
D828	Die junge Nonne
D957/2	Kriegers Ahnung
D957/8	Der Atlas

Again, detailed analysis of one example provides insight into works that lie at the dramatic end of the song spectrum.

"Die junge Nonne" (D828)

"Die junge Nonne" (D828), a Craigher setting composed in 1824 or early 1825, draws its subject from the legend of St. Agnes – a favorite Romantic theme.[1] On a stormy night, ensconced within the tower of a monastery, a young nun eagerly awaits the coming of her Savior. The vision of her impending marriage with Christ sends her into a state of ecstasy. Suddenly, the tolling of the tower bells announces His arrival. As the bells continue ringing, calling her up to heaven, the enraptured nun sings out a joyful Hallelujah. At last, the raging turmoil of life yields to the eternal comfort of death.

Ex. 39 Schubert, "Die junge Nonne" (D828), mm. 1–2

Given the dramatic presentational mode, depiction of action, and powerful imagery of the text, one might expect the nun's monologue to be set like a dramatic scene, with loosely alternating sections of accompanied recitative and arioso. It is not. Curiously, the setting includes some strophic repetition and displays a high degree of motivic unity. The entire piece grows out of the melodic/rhythmic motive presented in the first two measures of the piano introduction (Ex. 39). "Die junge Nonne" is in fact a mixed-genre Lied – a dramatic scene transformed by the inclusion of traditional Lied characteristics. The mixture of genre arises largely from the central role of metaphor in Craigher's text.

The poem (translation on pp. 147–148) comprises three five-line and one six-line stanzas:

1   Wie braust durch die Wipfel der heulende Sturm!
Es klirren die Balken – es zittert das Haus!
Es rollet der Donner – es leuchtet der Blitz! –
Und finster die Nacht, wie das Grab! –   –   –
Immerhin, immerhin!

6   So tobt' es auch jüngst noch in mir!
Es brauste das Leben, wie jetzo der Sturm!
Es bebten die Glieder, wie jetzo das Haus!
Es flammte die Liebe, wie jetzo der Blitz! –
Und finster die Brust, wie das Grab! –

11   Nun tobe du wilder, gewaltiger Sturm!
Im Herzen ist Friede, im Herzen ist Ruh! –
Des Bräutigams harret die liebende Braut,
Gereinigt in prüfender Glut –
Der ewigen Liebe getraut. –

16   Ich harre, mein Heiland, mit sehnendem Blick;
Komm, himmlischer Bräutigam, hole die Braut!
Erlöse die Seele von irdischer Haft! –
Horch! friedlich ertönet das Glöcklein vom Thurm;
Es lockt mich das süße Getön
Allmächtig zu ewigen Höhn –
"Alleluja!"

118

The first poetic stanza focuses on the external aspects of the scene. In a series of short parallel phrases, the nun describes the effects of the storm which rages about her: the howling of the wind, the clattering of the rafters, the rumbling of thunder, the flash of lightning. Craigher's excessive punctuation contributes to the impression of tension and turmoil. Both the abundance of dashes and the use of exclamation points for each line-ending help convey the turbulence of this wild night vision. But the nun's description of the tempest is not objective or dispassionate. Her yearning spirit is manifest in the final line of the stanza: "Immerhin, immerhin!"

The second stanza highlights the metaphorical relationship between the present storm and the nun's previous emotional state: "So tobt' es noch jüngst auch in mir!" Each image from the first stanza – the storm, the house, the lightning, the grave – finds a direct counterpart in the second. Just as the storm rages, so did her life; just as the house trembles, so did her limbs; just as the lightning flashes, so did her love. Most importantly, just as the night is now dark as a tomb, so, not long ago, was the nun's heart.

Craigher underscores this metaphorical relation through structural parallels between the two stanzas. Both lines 1–4 and lines 7–10 conclude with the words "Sturm," "Haus," "Blitz," and "Grab." The last lines of these two line-groupings are almost identical ("Und finster die Nacht/Brust, wie das Grab!"). Moreover, both groupings have the same syllable (11–11–11–8) and stress (4–4–4–3) patterns. These corresponding line-groupings do not comprise full stanzas. Nor do they occur in the same position within their respective stanzas. The first starts at the beginning of the stanza, while the second starts one line into the stanza. The two halves of the metaphor (or, more precisely, simile) are separated by a kind of interlude, formed by lines 5 and 6. This difference in positioning, as we will see, has significant implications for Schubert's musical setting.

In the third stanza, the nun rejects the storm metaphor as no longer appropriate. Whereas previously her heart had been full of turmoil, now it is peaceful: "Im Herzen ist Friede, im Herzen ist Ruh!" The raging storm has lost significance, for she is purified and vowed to eternal love. Although the third stanza is clearly set apart from the metaphorical unit of the first two stanzas, it maintains a subtle connection through word repetition. The first line of the third stanza repeats the verb "toben" in the same position as the first line of the second stanza (compare lines 6 and 11). Similarly, line 11 ends with the word "Sturm," as do both lines 1 and 7 (which begin the two four-line groupings mentioned above). Again, these connections have important musical implications, which will be discussed later.

The fourth stanza contains the central dramatic event. First, the nun addresses her Savior, calling upon him to loosen her earthly bonds. Lines 16–18 thus essentially continue the thought of stanza 3. At the beginning of line 19, however, it becomes apparent that something has happened: the tower bells have begun to ring. The nun's exclamation "Horch!" suggests that this event occurs just before the start of line 19 – during the pause indicated by the dash after "Haft."

The dramatic action of the fourth stanza has, of course, a metaphorical meaning. Just as the storm symbolizes the nun's previous emotional turmoil, so the tolling of the bells symbolizes the arrival of death. Lines 20 and 21 ("Es lockt mich das süße Getön / Allmächtig zu ewigen Höhn"), describing the nun's ascent to heaven, are presumably spoken while she is dying. The final word of the poem ("Alleluja"), which Craigher places in quotation marks, seems to represent a different kind of discourse altogether; it is apparently pronounced *after* the nun has died. One might imagine the word as belonging to one or more other speakers – perhaps a choir of angels.

Although the fourth stanza is distinguished from the others by its portrayal of action, there are, once again, several connections. As mentioned above, the first three lines of the fourth stanza essentially continue the thought of the third stanza. There is also a structural parallel between the third and fourth stanzas. Specifically, both stanzas contain two consecutive three-stress lines (14–15, 20–21) that contrast with the preceding four-stress lines. As with the first and second stanzas, these corresponding line-groupings do not occur in the same place within the stanza. In the third stanza, the three-stress pair comes at the end of the stanza, while in the fourth stanza it comes one line before the end. Not surprisingly, this structural parallel helps to shape Schubert's setting.

The nun's spiritual renewal finds musical expression through a variety of compositional techniques. Most obvious is the modal shift from f minor to F major that occurs at the beginning of the third stanza (m. 51). Foreshadowed in the setting of the wistful line "Immerhin, immerhin!" (mm. 31–33), the change of mode reflects the change of mood expressed in the text. The major mode, which persists through the rest of the song, helps convey the nun's newly "uplifted" spirit.

The action of the poem is also reflected in the gradual transformation of the harmonic language. For the first two stanzas (with the exception of lines 5–6), Schubert writes in a heavily chromatic idiom. In lines 1–4, the harmonic progression arises from chromatic linear motion – first ascending,

Ex. 40 Harmonic reduction of "Die junge Nonne" (D828), mm. 8–28 then descending (Ex. 40). The harmony reaches a climax at the word "finster," with a half-diminished seventh over G♯ (m. 22). This dissonant sonority, as well as the falling diminished fifth in the bass, makes the evil of the night clearly audible.

Ex. 41 Harmonic reduction of "Die junge Nonne" (D828), mm. 52–61

The third stanza, in which the nun rejects the storm metaphor, is primarily diatonic. The harmony involves standard progressions (Ex. 41). In mm. 52–55, the harmony modulates from F to C (though not in root position), via a secondary dominant. Despite the unexpected resolution of the A major harmony of m. 56 to V_7/IV, rather than to vi, the impression created by the third stanza, particularly in contrast to the preceding music, is that of harmonic simplicity. This is appropriate, for the nun now experiences an inward calm.

The fourth stanza encapsulates the shift from chromatic to diatonic writing (Ex. 42). In mm. 62–68, the mounting intensity of the poetic lines is reflected musically through an ascending chromatic progression from F to D♭, or I to ♭VI. After the return to the tonic in mm. 69–74, the succeeding

Ex. 42 Harmonic reduction of "Die junge Nonne" (D828), mm. 62–87

Ex. 43 Schubert, "Die junge Nonne" (D828), mm. 66–74

music is essentially diatonic. The last word of the poem, "Alleluja," is set to the simple cadential progression I–IV–V– I. All traces of chromaticism have vanished. The change of harmonic idiom – both within the fourth stanza and over the whole piece – illustrates the progression from earthly turmoil to heavenly peace.

The nun's struggle to escape her living bondage is also portrayed through the pitch structure of the vocal line. In the first (and second) stanza, the vocal line quickly establishes c", or scale-degree 5, as a primary tone. It then proceeds up chromatically through c♯" to d", as if striving to reach the tonic (mm. 10–19). But this motion is thwarted. The line slips back down chromatically to c" (mm. 22–28). The effect is one of frustrated effort.

In the third stanza, the vocal line, after first reestablishing the primary tone c", succeeds in breaking beyond the pitch d". In m. 54, the vocal line reaches e" just at the word "Friede," the first hint of the new poetic tone. Significantly, it repeats this pitch for the similarly suggestive words "Ruh," "Bräutigams," and "liebende." The vocal line does not rest here, however, instead proceeding up one more step to the climactic f' for "gereinigt," "Glut," and "getraut." Foreshadowed in bar 32 ("immerhin"), the arrival of the vocal line at the tonic pitch represents the fulfillment of a desire, the transition to a new emotional state.

The most important dramatic event in the poem is the nun's death, signaled by the ringing of the tower bells just before line 19. The poetic pause indicated by the dash after line 18 corresponds to the short instrumental interlude in mm. 68–69. It is during these bars that the bells ostensibly begin to ring. Schubert captures the magic of the moment with the striking resolution of an augmented sixth chord on ♭VI directly to the tonic. When the voice enters in m. 71, it picks up the diminished fifth interval contained in the augmented sixth harmony, and the progression is repeated (Ex. 43).[2]

While the musical setting illustrates the changes experienced by the poetic persona, the dramatic effect is tempered by the inclusion of certain traditional Lied traits. The song is not throughcomposed, as one might expect of a monologue, but rather involves a mixture of strophic form and through-composition. Moreover, as noted at the outset, the setting displays an extra-ordinarily high degree of motivic unity. There also are no modulations to speak of: the song remains firmly grounded in the tonic key (allowing for modal variation) throughout.

The mixture of strophic and throughcomposed elements is readily apparent in the following diagram of the musical form:

lines:	1–4	5–6	7–10	11–15	16–22
measure:	1	31	36	52	62
section:	A	coda	A'	B	C

Schubert begins the song with strophic repetitions. Measures 1–30, which set lines 1–4 of the poem, are essentially repeated in mm. 36–51, which set lines 7–10.[3] This musical repetition helps illustrate the metaphorical relations in the text. By giving lines 1–4 and 7–10 the same music, Schubert emphasizes the similarity between the storm and the nun's earlier emotional turmoil.

This is not, however, an example of pure or even modified strophic repe-tition, for, as noted earlier, the two line-groupings do not both begin their respective stanzas. Unlike nearly all strophic or modified strophic songs, the unit of repetition corresponds neither to a full stanza nor to the first part of one. Lines 5 and 6, around which the metaphor turns, are set as a short coda to the first stanza and are not repeated. Still, the *effect* is that of strophic repetition. In this song, a traditional Lied characteristic thus plays an important interpretive role. The musical repetition actualizes the meaning of the poetic metaphor.

After the second stanza, the song is mostly throughcomposed. There is one other instance of musical repetition: the expanded repetition of mm. 58–61 in mm. 76–83, presumably inspired by the structural parallels between lines 14–15 and 20–21 of the text. But because the repeated material comes at the end rather than at the beginning of the two stanzas, it does not sound like strophic repetition. The repetition is largely disguised.

The third stanza thus marks the beginning of a new structural principle. Interestingly, at m. 52, the third stanza opens like another strophic variation (now in the parallel major), but then quickly veers into new territory. The suggestion of continued strophic repetition was probably inspired by the structural parallels among lines 1, 7, and 11 of the text. Each of these lines ends with the word "Sturm." One is led to expect that line 11 will form the beginning of another line-grouping paralleling those of the first two stanzas (1–4, 7–10) and will have similar music. Perhaps more important than this word repetition, however, is the fact that line 11 refers back to the subject (i.e., the storm) of the first two stanzas. It is thus only natural for the setting of this line to refer back to earlier music.

The shift to throughcomposition marks the change of mood at the beginning of the third stanza. The deviation from strophic form after line 11 illustrates the nun's rejection of the storm metaphor. The music of the opening is no longer an appropriate means of expression. Just as the nun's thoughts take a new direction, so too does the music.

The striking motivic unity of the setting has several possible explanations. The opening two-measure melodic/rhythmic motive (or some slight variant) dominates the song. In no other dramatic Lied does Schubert approach this economy of means. One explanation might lie in the dactylic meter which persists throughout the poem. The rhythmic pattern of the opening motive is obviously well suited to this metrical arrangement.

Another explanation may be found in the metaphorical quality of the text. The storm is presented as an explicit metaphor for the nun's past emotional state. The ringing bells are presented as an implicit metaphor for the arrival of death. But perhaps death in this context should not be understood as a physiological event. One might regard death as symbolizing the nun's break with her emotional past, with life outside the monastery. Her ascent to heaven may be viewed as a metaphor for the new-found purity of her spiritual vows. From this perspective, there are no real dramatic events depicted in the poem; the action is all psychological.

This interpretation helps make sense of the lack of significant modulations in the setting. In dramatic scenes and ballads, the action is typically reflected in frequent and unexpected changes of key. The nun's monologue remains within the confines of a single key because the action takes place entirely within the mind of a single character.

Dramatic songs with admixtures of lyrical traits

Ultimately, the multiple layers of metaphorical meaning shift our focus from the external aspects of the scene to the spiritual transformation of the human subject. If one regards the song as an interior monologue – the private thoughts of a solitary character – the lyrical expression of motivic unity and harmonic stasis seems wholly appropriate.

9

Lyrico-dramatic songs

Schubert's most forward-looking Lieder are those which achieve a thorough fusion of lyricism and drama, with neither mode dominating. It is difficult, if not impossible, to identify the particular vocal traditions which merge in most of these works. We do not recognize them as spring songs, lullabies, laments, dramatic monologues, or ballads. Schubert creates a whole new manner of expression, combining aspects of dramatic declamation and lyrical song. In so doing, he anticipates the musical language of Hugo Wolf.

Various early songs employ a dramatic musical vocabulary in setting lyrical subjects. Such is the case with "Trost an Elisa" (D97) and "Die Sommernacht" (D289). The consoling sentiments expressed by the speaker in the first song and the quiet contemplation of the speaker in the second are set almost entirely in recitative. Schubert achieves a similar lyrico-dramatic effect in "Todtenopfer" (D101) and "Vergebliche Liebe" (D177), again dating from the mid 1810s.

"Viola" (D786) and "Vergißmeinnicht" (D792), composed in 1823 to texts by Schubert's friend Franz von Schober, also combine lyrical subjects with a dramatic musical language, but in quite a different way. Subtitled "Blumenballade," the two songs tell stories full of drama and pathos in which delicate blossoms and the forces of nature are cast as the central characters. While the poetic personae, refrains, and musical style recall the gentle world of Frühlingslieder, the narrative mode, throughcomposed forms, text-painting, and large proportions are reminiscent of the dramatic ballad. Lyricism and drama are evenly balanced. As John Reed has observed, the songs may be regarded as "a conscious attempt on the part of Schubert and Schober to give to the extended episodic song a new unity and strength, and so to make it a viable concert form."[1]

"Der Doppelgänger" (D957/13) represents one of Schubert's most sophisticated attempts to combine drama and lyricism within a song. In Heine's text, the past conflates with the present, reviving and/or revealing in the speaker the emotional turmoil of days long gone. During the first stanza, the speaker assumes the posture of an objective observer, pointing out the house of his former beloved. With the appearance of the speaker's ghostly double in the second stanza, it becomes evident that the wounds of the past still torture him. The Doppelgänger, wringing his hands in an exaggerated gesture of agony, apes not only his former self but his present self as well. Like the house, the speaker still stands in the same place; he still anguishes over his lost love. The drama of the song lies in the speaker's (and the listener's) gradual realization that nothing has changed. Both the vocal line, a pseudo-declamatory, quasi-monotone with increasing hints of melody, and the passacaglia-like accompaniment, marked by ever richer and more striking harmonies, capture the thorough blending of drama and lyricism in Heine's extraordinary poem.

Songs like "Gruppe aus dem Tartarus" (D583), "Grenzen der Menschheit" (D716), "Freiwilliges Versinken" (D700), and "Der Doppelgänger" (D957/13) resist attempts to uncover their precise generic origins. They also resist successful performance. The sublimity of thought and feeling, one senses, is essentially unrealizable through the medium of voice and piano. These supremely complex mixed-genre Lieder, composed in a musical language far in advance of its time, pointed the way to a new world of vocal expression.

A selective list of works that may be described as lyrico-dramatic songs appears below.

Lyrico-dramatic songs

D97	Trost, an Elisa
D101	Todtenopfer
D142	Geistesgruß
D177	Vergebliche Liebe
D215a, 216	Meerestille
D289	Die Sommernacht
D583	Gruppe aus dem Tartarus
D700	Freiwilliges Versinken
D708	Im Walde
D716	Grenzen der Menschheit
D737	An die Leier
D786	Viola
D792	Vergißmeinnicht
D795/12	Pause
D807	Auflösung
D927	Vor meiner Wiege
D957/11	Die Stadt
D957/13	Der Doppelgänger

Once more, we turn to a specific example to aid our understanding of the works located in the middle of the song spectrum.

"Pause" (D795/12)

"Pause," the twelfth song in *Die schöne Müllerin*, marks the dramatic (though not numerical) center of the cycle.[2] Here a new tragic undertone emerges, signaling the sorry change of fortune that awaits the poor miller. "Pause" thus functions as a pivot or turning point in the musical narrative. In the preceding songs, as the miller falls in love with the maiden, he becomes increasingly jubilant; in the succeeding songs, when she spurns him, his spirits plummet.[3]

As the title suggests, "Pause" also functions as a kind of interlude or narrative break which disrupts the dramatic and musical continuity of the cycle. "Ich kann nicht mehr singen, mein Herz ist zu voll, / Weiß nicht, wie ich's in Reime zwingen soll." Claiming he can no longer sing, the miller adopts a declamatory vocal style, at times verging on recitative, that contrasts sharply with the preceding Lieder. The effect is that of a dramatic soliloquy, poised on the edge of speech and song. Whether the miller will resume his musical narrative, whether the "pause" in action is indeed just that rather than a permanent break, is the fundamental question underlying this unusual Lied.

Here drama and lyricism are inextricably intertwined. The miller says he cannot sing; in fact, he doesn't want to. By not singing, he hopes indefinitely to sustain his present moment of bliss. Singing would imply a resumption of the narrative, possibly leading to an unhappy outcome. Thus the usual association of speech and song with drama and lyricism, respectively, is turned on its head. Speaking (i.e., not singing) amounts to a lyrical suspension of time, while singing suggests the furthering of dramatic action. However, the reverse relation is also true. Interrupting the song cycle is a dramatic event; continuing with additional Lieder suggests a return of lyricism. This thorough fusion of poetic modes inspired one of Schubert's most ingenious mixed-genre Lieder.

A few preliminary observations about the song text are useful to an understanding of the musical setting. Wilhelm Müller's poem (translation on p. 148) divides into two stanzas of unequal length – ten and eight lines, respectively. The lines are grouped in rhyming pairs:

1	Meine Laute hab' ich gehängt an die Wand,
	Hab' sie umschlungen mit einem grünen Band –
3	Ich kann nicht mehr singen, mein Herz ist zu voll,
	Weiß nicht, wie ich's in Reime zwingen soll.
5	Meiner Sehnsucht allerheißesten Schmerz
	Durft' ich aushauchen in Liederscherz,
7	Und wie ich klagte so süß und fein,
	Glaubt' ich doch, mein Leiden wär nicht klein.
9	Ei, wie groß ist wohl meines Glückes Last,
	Daß kein Klang auf Erden es in sich fasst?
11	Nun, liebe Laute, ruh' an dem Nagel hier!
	Und weht ein Lüftchen über die Saiten dir,
13	Und streift eine Biene mit ihren Flügeln dich,
	Da wird mir so bange und es durchschauert mich.

15   Warum ließ ich das Band auch hängen so lang?
      Oft fliegt's um die Saiten mit seufzendem Klang.
17   Ist es der Nachklang meiner Liebespein?
      Soll es das Vorspiel neuer Lieder sein?

Several aspects of the poem are unconventional. First, both of the poetic stanzas are far longer than the typical quatrains of Lied verses. While the punctuation of lines 1–8 (and also perhaps 11–14) suggests internal four-line groupings which might be perceived as quatrains, this structure is not supported by the physical layout of Müller's text.

In addition, many of the poetic lines in "Pause" contain five stressed syllables, rather than the usual three or four. As Ann Fehn and Rufus Hallmark have shown, pentameter verse appears infrequently in Schubert's song texts.[4] It occurs primarily in odes (especially those of Klopstock and Matthisson) and classical monologues and dialogues (particularly by Schiller). In these songs, Schubert uses both uneven and even rhythmic declamation. Uneven declamation often yields four-measure phrasing. The rhythm of the pentameter line somewhere accelerates so that two stressed syllables fall within a single measure. In even declamation, on the other hand, each stressed syllable receives equal metrical weight, producing irregular phrasing. It is this second type of declamation that Schubert employs through most of "Pause." As we shall see, the irregular phrasing at the entrance of the vocal line has interpretive significance.

"Pause" displays what might loosely be described as "modified strophic" form. It comprises two large musical sections, or "strophes," corresponding to the two large poetic stanzas. Both stanzas are introduced by the same accompanimental music (though only the first four measures of the eight-measure piano introduction reappear before the second stanza) and begin in a nearly identical manner.[5] After the third line of each stanza, the close musical similarity between them disappears. Example 44 presents a diagram of the musical form.[6]

Ex. 44 Musical form of Schubert's "Pause" (D795/12)

I					II				
line no.:									
1	3	5	7	9	11	13	15	17	
a_1 a_1 a_2 a'_1		b_1 b_2 b'_1 b'_2		c_1 c_2 $\widehat{c_2}$	a_1 a_1 a'_2 c'_1		a''_1 a''_1 d_1 d_2 $\widehat{d_1 \; d_2}$		
A		B		C	A'		D		

⌢ = textual repeat

129

While the two large musical strophes end differently, there are never-theless several interesting parallels between their concluding gestures. Both stanzas gradually slip into a kind of recitative, with the voice declaiming freely over a chordal accompaniment. In the first stanza, this occurs in mm. 33–35 (the opening of the C section). In the second, it occurs in mm. 54–55 (the end of the A' section) and bars 64–66 and 72–74 (the end of the D section).[7]

In addition, while the large-scale harmonic progressions of the two stanzas differ fundamentally (stanza 1: I–V; stanza 2: I–I), both stanzas employ an increasingly complex harmonic vocabulary. The first stanza begins in the tonic, moves abruptly to the key of the submediant (m. 20), then to the super-tonic (m. 26), and finally to the dominant (m. 32) – a standard progression. In the C section, however, there is a temporary excursion to the remote key of D♭ before the half-cadence, via an augmented sixth, on the dominant (mm. 39–40). The second stanza also begins by moving from the tonic to the submediant (mm. 52–53) and then to the supertonic (m. 55). The music then shifts suddenly to a remote harmonic plane: the key of A♭ major, or ♭VII of the original tonic. The route back to the dominant for the final cadence is circuitous. Through linear motion, the A♭ harmony leads to the even more remote region of F♭ before finally arriving at the preparatory augmented sixth.[8] As if to confirm this unusual progression, Schubert repeats the entire passage (with the addition of an extra measure).

Is there a textual basis for these points of similarity between the two stanzas – the declamatory vocal style and the increasingly complex harmonic vocabulary? It seems significant that both stanzas end with questions (whose effect in the song is intensified through textual repeats). The uncertainty implied by those questions is expressed in an experimental musical language. Further insight into the text–music relationship requires close examination of the individual sections of the song.

"Pause" begins with a rounded eight-measure piano introduction, divided evenly into groups of four plus four measures (Ex. 45). The striking rhythmic/

Ex. 45 Schubert, "Pause" (D795/12), mm. 1–4

melodic motive of m. 1 (soon to be associated with the sound of the lute but as yet unidentified) recurs in mm. 2, 5 and 6, supporting the balanced phrase structure. The tonic pedal, which briefly gives way to the dominant near the end of each four-measure phrase, is likewise mysterious. Its effect, however, is that of restraint, steadfastness, perhaps even monotony.

In the first vocal section of the song (mm. 9–19, A in the structural diagram given above), the meaning of these various musical features becomes clear. The miller announces that he has hung his lute on the wall and draped a green ribbon around it; he is so overcome with emotion that he can no longer continue singing. The keyboard music (mm. 9–14, 17–19), derived from m. 1 and mm. 3–4, is now recognizable as a stylization of a lute accompaniment. It serves as an emblem of the miller's lute, dangling idly on the wall.[9]

The miller's claim that he can no longer sing is supported by the music in several ways. The tonic pedal, which persists throughout the section with the exception of just two measures (15–16), creates an impression of musical stasis or rigidity. In addition, Schubert gives the vocal line a square chordal melody that clings to the notes of the tonic triad, essentially going nowhere (Ex. 46). The avoidance of sweeping melodic gestures and the monotony of the three-fold repetition suggest a mode of expression closer to speech than to song. This impression is supported by the irregular two-and-a-half measure vocal phrasing that results from even declamation of the pentameter lines.[10] Following the regular eight-measure period of the piano introduction, this phrasing has a particularly strange and unnatural effect, which might be interpreted as "unmusical." The miller's claim to have put his instrument aside and assumed a speaking voice is reinforced.[11]

The second section (mm. 20–33, B in Ex. 44) presents a striking contrast to the first, arising from the shift in poetic focus. The miller thinks back to former days of painful longing and remembers how he could then express himself in song. To represent these memories, the B section assumes a more "musical" character than the A section. The voice and piano no longer work at cross-purposes. Instead, they move in parallel thirds, as if the singer

Ex. 46 Schubert, "Pause" (D795/12), mm. 9–11

Ex. 47 Schubert, "Pause" (D795/12), mm. 20–26

were accompanying himself on the lute (Ex. 47). The notion of "Sehnsucht" is expressed in the sighing eighth-note motives of the vocal melody as well as the minor mode, and the very mention of music-making ("Durft' ich aushauchen in Liederscherz") inspires an exuberant melodic flourish (mm. 24–26). Throughout the section, the vocal line displays a greater vitality and more conventional melodic shape than it had previously. The bass line, too, involves more motion, producing greater harmonic activity than the static pedal point of the A section. Even the internal phrase structure (b1 b2 b'1 b'2) has a more Lied-like character than the monotonous repetitions heard earlier.[12] All of these features suggest that misery and painful longing are appropriate subjects for musical expression.

There is something perplexing about the use of the word "Liederscherz." Why the suggestion of jollity and playfulness? Schubert himself may have thought Müller's word choice odd, for the musical manuscript substitutes the word "Liederschmerz." According to Maximilian and Lilly Schochow, however, this represents a simple copying mistake, not a deliberate change.[13] The musical setting supports their view, for it conveys an impression of lightheartedness. Both the sprightly dotted rhythms of the piano's left hand in m. 23 and the transition to the major mode suggest that the miller may not have been so unhappy after all. In stating "Und wie ich klagte so süß und fein, / Glaubt' ich doch, mein Leiden wär' nicht klein," the miller seems to mock his previous misery. Once he had thought the burden not small! Now (so the lines imply) he sees just how insignificant it really was.

In the third section of the song (mm. 33–41, C in the diagram), the ambiguity deepens. The two lines of text form a rhetorical question: how great is the burden of my [the miller's] happiness if no earthly music can contain it? Clearly the miller seeks no answer; he uses the rhetorical question as a means to convey the measure of his present happiness. This section appropriately ends on a half-cadence. Just as the rhetorical question requires no response, so the dominant harmony requires no resolution. It forms the conclusion of the phrase.[14]

Yet what is one to make of the phrase "Glückes Last"? Lines 7–10 of the text suggest that the miller's present happiness represents a far greater burden than the painful longing of the past. If so, is this larger burden better suited to musical expression? What is it that distinguishes the present from the past – the miller's blissful infatuation from his lovesick desire? The C section represents a turning point in the song. Beneath the surface of exuberant optimism runs an undercurrent of doubt. The miller begins to suspect the direction of his fate.

The fourth section of the song (mm. 46–55, A' in the diagram), marking the start of the second poetic stanza, is a variation of the first section. After a repeat of the first four measures of the piano introduction, the voice enters with essentially the same music as the opening of the song. While the first two phrases (mm. 46–51) are nearly identical with the earlier music, the third phrase (mm. 52–53) is transposed up a whole step. The fourth phrase differs sharply from the corresponding passage in the first section; this declamatory statement instead bears a strong resemblance to the opening of the C section (mm. 33–35).

That the fourth section begins like the first is understandable, given the similarity between the opening lines of the two stanzas (lines 1 and 11). In both, the miller focuses on the lute hanging on the wall. Line 11, however, takes the form of an imperative. Doubting the reality of his happiness, he distances himself from the musical instrument. Succumbing to its seductive entreaties would presumably imply the return of his previous misery. The repetition of music from the A section suggests the miller's effort to recapture the mood of the opening, to cast away his doubts about the future.

The sudden deviation from the A section material and the unexpected cadence on the supertonic (m. 55), however, belie the miller's forced optimism. The emotional turmoil he experiences at the thought that the lute might play music by itself is aptly expressed through the declamatory vocal line of mm. 54–55, leading to the minor cadence.

In the fifth section (mm. 56–77, D in the diagram), the miller's fear is realized: the lute makes music of its own. Chastizing himself for draping such a long ribbon around the instrument, the miller ponders the significance of the sighing sound it makes while brushing the strings. "Ist es der Nachklang meiner Liebespein? / Soll es das Vorspiel neuer Lieder sein?"

The D section begins with music drawn once again from the A section: its first two phrases (mm. 56–62) are a variation of mm. 9–14, sounded in the remote key of A♭ major. From one perspective, this unexpected harmonic event appears to be a musical parallel for the miller's increasing disorientation. Just as the harmony jumps suddenly from one key area to the next (ii to ♭VII), so the miller's thoughts fly in unexpected directions, leading him to the brink of despair. The strange A♭ harmony might also be viewed as belonging to the mysterious realm of "natural" music – that produced by non-human agents such as the wind, bees' wings, or a rustling ribbon.[15]

Ex. 48 Schubert, "Pause" (D795/12), mm. 63–69

The second half of the D section, comprising the two questions, diverges from the A section material. The miller's initial enthusiasm has vanished, opening the door to doubt and uncertainty. Schubert sets the first question in a declamatory and discordant manner, reflecting the meaning of "Liebespein." The second question, by contrast, is given a metrically regular, diatonic tune, mimicking the sound of "neuer Lieder" (Ex. 48). These two questions, unlike the one posed at the end of the first stanza, are not rhetorical: the miller desperately wants to know the answers. Significantly, there is no half-cadence this time. The dissonant chord on the downbeat of m. 66 (and later m. 74) is reinterpreted as a German sixth and leads to a full cadence.

It is crucial to recognize that these questions do not fall into an "either–or" pattern. The answer to *both* questions, as the rest of the song cycle bears out, is "yes"; the miller's painful longing returns, and a sequence of new Lieder follows. To discover this answer, it is not necessary to hear out the cycle, for there are several important clues within the actual framework of the song.

The tonic cadences in mm. 69 and 71 make the poetic line "Soll es das Vorspiel neuer Lieder sein?" sound more like a statement than a question. The vocal line does not end on a raised pitch, as one would expect with a question, but rather descends to the tonic. Moreover, the return to the original tonic harmony suggests that the answer to the questions is somehow contained in the beginning of the song. Although the miller says that he has put his instrument aside because he is too ecstatic to sing, he nevertheless expresses himself through song. We now know that he cannot do otherwise, for his happiness is only an illusion. (The miller himself begins to suspect this midway through the piece.)

Another important clue lies in the piano postlude (mm. 78–81). These four measures are a slightly varied repetition of mm. 5–8, the second half of the piano introduction (and the very measures that are missing from the accompanimental introduction to the second stanza). By framing the main body of the song with the first and second halves of the introduction, Schubert makes "Pause" into a kind of expanded Vorspiel; the whole piece may be viewed as a "prelude to new songs." Significantly, the very next song in the cycle, "Mit dem grünen Lautenbande," is in the same key (B♭ major) as "Pause."[16] It thus makes sense to regard "Pause" as a prelude to the following music.[17]

The miller's suspicions turn out to be correct. Just two songs later, the hunter arrives on the scene, ready to snatch away his precious love. New songs follow, leading to the sorrowful outcome. But is this outcome really so sorrowful after all? For the miller himself, there can be no doubt. But the listener has had the benefit of hearing the rest of the cycle. In this sense, the resumption of the musical narrative after "Pause" has been a good thing. Schubert plays upon this dual interpretation of events in the final bars of the song. The teasing mode switch from major to minor and back to major again in mm. 78–81 (Ex. 49), like a musical wink, suggests that all may in fact be for the best.[18]

Ex. 49 Schubert, "Pause" (D795/12), mm. 78–81

Conclusion

Schubert's song output does not follow any straight line of development from simple to complex works. A number of the early songs, such as "Gretchen am Spinnrade" (D118), "Schäfers Klagelied" (D121), and "Erlkönig" (D328), show a high level of compositional artistry while various late settings, such as "An Sylvia" (D891) and "Eine altschottische Ballade" (D923), are far less intricate. Nevertheless, a general trend may be observed: the maturation of Schubert's compositional technique in song-writing involved the gradual movement away from distinct subgenres of the Lied toward a fusion of vocal kinds.

With the early songs of the mid 1810s, it is generally easy to identify the type of work represented. The songs fall into recognizable categories, characterized by a variety of traits. Thus "Stimme der Liebe" (D187) is a love song, "Amphiaraos" (D166) a dramatic ballad, "Grablied" (D218) a funeral dirge, and "Bundeslied" (D258) a drinking song. Schubert also writes romances, hymns, lullabies, nocturnes, barcarolles, serenades, folk ballads, laments, work songs, cantatas, spring songs, and dramatic scenes.

The later songs tend to resist categorization by subgenre. Many of the settings dating from the 1820s exemplify a subtle mixture of genre traits, combining dramatic, narrative, and lyrical elements. During this phase of his career Schubert became most absorbed by the endless varieties of modified strophic form, which combines static and dynamic impulses. These mature songs are best described as "mixed-genre Lieder," or even perhaps simply as "Lieder."

This gradual transformation of genre was necessitated by the Romantic poetry to which Schubert became increasingly attracted after 1819. The poetic personae in songs such as Müller's "Einsamkeit" (D911/12) and Heine's "Der Doppelgänger" (D957/13) possess a psychological depth unknown to the stereotypical protagonists of early settings, such as Kosegarten's "Schwanengesang" (D318), Salis-Seewis's "Fischerlied" (D351), and Matthisson's "Stimme der Liebe" (D418). But these poetic personae are not fully identifiable characters, like those in "Szene aus Faust" (D126), "Iphigenia" (D573), or "Prometheus" (D674). The Müller and Heine poems steer a middle course between lyrical sentiment and dramatic action: of central importance here is the protagonist's psychological development.

Conclusion

Schubert captures this new poetic sensibility by combining dramatic and lyrical elements within a song. Dramatic musical gestures used to portray specific characters in the dramatic scenes and ballads of the mid-1810s add depth to the anonymous poetic personae of the later settings. Similarly, traits initially used to depict action, such as throughcomposed form and meandering harmonic schemes, later help convey psychological changes. This fusion of genres marks Schubert's most important legacy to nineteenth-century song composition.

Schubert's dramatic songs – both the *dramatic scenes* and *dramatic ballads*, as well as the more complex *mixed-genre Lieder* – demonstrate the importance of genre to interpretation. Measured against the traditional strophic Lied, these songs seem bizarre. The use of progressive tonality, declamatory vocal lines, throughcomposed forms, irregular phrasing, accompanimental text-painting, and frequent changes of meter, tempo, and texture stands in sharp contrast to the musical conventions associated with traditional song types such as the Frühlingslied, Ständchen, or Wiegenlied. The use of dramatic subjects is likewise foreign to Volkslieder. If, as with many of Schubert's contemporaries, strophic (or perhaps modified strophic) form, tonal unity, musical regularity, and lyrical subjects are viewed as the mark of a successful Lied, then Schubert's dramatic songs must be judged failures.

For Schubert's dramatic songs to be appreciated, they must be analyzed in context. They should be studied not only in relation to Volkslieder, with which they share just a few traits, but in relation to many dramatic vocal genres of the late eighteenth and early nineteenth centuries. Before a particular song can be understood and evaluated, we must know what kind of a work it represents, i.e., what musical traditions or compositional conventions it engages. Without recognizing the genre (or fusion of genres in the later settings), we cannot understand how these songs communicate meaning.

While this is particularly so for Schubert's dramatic songs, whose unusual aspects tend to mystify, the same holds true for the many other genres in his Lied oeuvre. Every act of interpretation requires some familiarity with the work's type or kind. Genre studies of other song types thus represent an important area for future research. Here, genre is understood neither as an abstract ideal type nor merely as a convenient taxonomic tool. Instead, it signifies a conventional function or use of language (both poetic and musical) as evidenced by a series of actual compositions. Genre studies focus on similarities between works – the patterns of convention necessary for the communication of meaning. Studies of this kind shed light on songs that remain in undeserved obscurity and enhance our appreciation of this wealth of music.

APPENDIX

English translations of song texts

Group from Tartarus (D583)

Listen – like the murmur of the angry sea,
Like a brook weeping through the rocky hollows,
Rises yonder a low, heavy, empty,
    Tortured groan!

    Pain distorts
Their faces, despair opens wide
    Their jaws in perpetual curse.
Hollow are their eyes – their gaze
Fixes anxiously on the bridge over Cocytus,
    Following, weeping, the river's mournful course.

They ask each other, fearfully, softly,
Whether the end is near.
Eternity swings over them in circles,
    Breaking Saturn's scythe in two.

Lullaby (D527)

The woods exhort, the river cries out:
"Sweet boy, come to us!"
The boy approaches, marvels and tarries,
And is healed of all pain.

The quail's song echoes from the bushes,
The day makes play with shimmering colours;
On flowers red and blue
The moist dew of heaven glistens.

He lies down in the cool grass
And lets the clouds drift above him;
Nestling close to his mother,
He is lulled to sleep by the god of dreams.

    (Translation from: Richard Wigmore, *Schubert: The Complete Song Texts* [New York, 1988], 310–311)

Appendix

Scene from Faust (D126)

Cathedral

[*Organ and anthem. Gretchen in the congregation. An Evil Spirit whispers to her over her shoulder*]

Evil Spirit. How different it all was
Gretchen, when you came here
All innocent to the altar,
Out of the worn-out little book
Lisping your prayers,
Half a child's game,
Half God in the heart!
Gretchen!
How is your head?
And your heart –
What are its crimes?
Do you pray for your mother's soul, who
thanks to you
And your sleeping draught overslept into a
long, long pain?
And whose blood stains your threshold?
Yes, and already under your heart
Does it not grow and quicken
And torture itself and you
With its foreboding presence?

Gretchen Alas! Alas!
If I could get rid of the thoughts
Which course through my head hither and thither
Despite me!

Choir. Dies irae, dies illa
Solvet saeclum in favilla.
[*The organ plays*]

Evil Spirit. Agony seizes you!
The trumpet sounds!
The graves tremble
And your heart
From its ashen rest
To fiery torment
Comes up recreated
Trembling too!

Gretchen. Oh to escape from here!
I feel as if the organ
Were stifling me,
And the music dissolving
My heart in its depths.

140

Choir.   Judex ergo cum sedebit,
           Quidquid latet adparebit,
           Nil inultum remanebit.

Gretchen.   I cannot breathe!
              The pillars of the walls
              Are round my throat!
              The vaulted roof
              Chokes me! – Air!

Evil Spirit.   Hide yourself! Nor sin nor shame
                 Remains hidden.
                 Air? Light?
                 Woe to you!

Choir.   Quid sum miser tunc dicturus?
           Quem patronum rogaturus?
           Cum vix justus sit securus.

Evil Spirit.   The blessed turn
                 Their faces from you.
                 The pure shudder
                 To reach out their hands to you.
                 Woe!

Choir.   Quid sum miser tunc dicturus?

Gretchen.   Neighbor! Help! Your smelling bottle!
              [*She faints*]

> (Translation from: Louis MacNeice, ed.,
> *Goethe's Faust*, Parts I and II [New York,
> 1951; reprint, 1976], 128–130)

Death and the Maiden (D531)

Maiden:
Pass me by, oh, pass me by!
Go, fierce skeleton!
I am still young; go, dear!
And do not touch me.

Death:
Give me your hand, you fair and gentle creature.
I am a friend and do not come to punish.
Be of good cheer. I am not fierce.
You shall sleep softly in my arms.

141

Appendix

The Diver (D77)

"Who will dare, knight or squire
To dive into this abyss?
I hurl this golden goblet down,
The black mouth has already devoured it.
He who can show me the goblet again
May keep it, it is his."

Thus the king speaks, and from the top
Of the cliff, which juts abruptly and steeply
Into the infinite sea,
He hurls the goblet into the howling Charybdis.
"Who is there brave enough, I ask once more,
To dive down into the depths?"

And the knights and squires around him
Listen, and keep silent,
Looking down into the turbulent sea,
And none desires to win the goblet.
And the king asks a third time:
"Is there no one who will dare the depths?"

Yet all remain as silent as before;
Then a young squire, gentle and bold,
Steps from the hesitant throng,
Throws off his belt and his cloak.
And all the men and women around him
Gaze in astonishment at the fine youth.

And as he steps to the cliff's edge
And looks down into the abyss,
The waters which Charybdis devoured
She now regurgitates, roaring,
And, as if with the rumbling of distant thunder,
They rush foaming from the black womb.

The waters seethe and boil, rage and hiss
As if they were mixed with fire,
The steaming spray gushes up to the heavens,
And flood piles on flood, ceaselessly,
Never exhausting itself, never emptying,
As if the sea would beget another sea.

But at length the turbulent force abates,
And black from the white foam
A yawning rift gapes deep down,
Bottomless, as if it led to hell's domain,
And you see the tumultuous foaming waves,
Sucked down into the seething crater.

142

Appendix

Now swiftly, before the surge returns,
The youth commends himself to God,
And – a cry of horror is heard all around –
The whirlpool has already borne him away,
And over the bold swimmer, mysteriously,
the gaping abyss closes; he will never be seen again.

Calm descends over the watery abyss.
Only in the depths is there a hollow roar,
And the words falter from mouth to mouth:
"Valiant youth, farewell!"
The roar grows ever more hollow,
And they wait, anxious and fearful.

Even if you threw in the crown itself,
And said: "Whoever brings me this crown
Shall wear it and be king" –
I would not covet the precious reward.
What the howling depths may conceal
No living soul will ever tell.

Many a vessel, caught by the whirlpool,
Has plunged sheer into the depths,
Yet only wrecked keels and masts
Have struggled out of the all-consuming grave.
Like the rushing of a storm,
The roaring grows ever closer and more vivid.

The waters seethe and boil, rage and hiss,
As if they were mixed with fire;
The steaming spray gushes up to the heavens
And flood piles on flood, ceaselessly,
And, as if with the rumbling of distant thunder,
the waters rush foaming from the black womb.

But look! From the black watery womb
A form rises, as white as a swan,
An arm and a glistening neck are revealed,
Rowing powerfully, and with energetic zeal,
It is he! And high in his left hand
He joyfully waves the goblet.

He breathes long, he breathes deeply,
And greets the heavenly light.
Rejoicing they call to each other:
"He's alive! He's here! The abyss did not keep him!"
From the grave, the swirling watery cavern,
The brave man has saved his living soul."

He approaches, the joyous throng surround him,
And he falls down at the king's feet,
Kneeling, he hands him the goblet,
And the king signals to his charming daughter,
Who fills it to the brim with sparkling wine;
Then the youth turned to the king:

"Long live the king! Rejoice,
Whoever breathes this rosy light!
But down below it is terrible,
And man should never tempt the gods
Nor ever desire to see
What they graciously conceal in night and horror.

"It tore me down as fast as lightning –
Then, from a rocky shaft
A torrential flood poured towards me:
I was seized by the double current's raging force,
And, like the giddy whirling of a top,
It hurled me round; I could not resist.

"Then God, to whom I cried,
Showed me, at the height of my dire distress,
A rocky reef, rising from the depths,
I swiftly gripped it and escaped death –
And there, too, the goblet hung on coral lips,
Or else it would have fallen into the bottomless ocean.

"For below me still it lay, fathomlessly deep,
There in purple darkness,
And even if, for the ear, there was eternal calm here,
The eye looked down with dread,
At the salamanders and dragons
Swarming in the terrifying caverns of hell.

"Black, in a ghastly mêlée,
Massed in horrifying clumps,
Teemed the stinging roach, the fish of the cliffs,
The hammer-head, hideously misshapen,
And, threatening me with his wrathful teeth,
The gruesome shark, the hyena of the sea.

"And there I hung, terrifyingly conscious
How far I was from human help,
Among larvae the only living heart,
Alone in terrible solitude,
Deep beneath the sound of human speech
With the monsters of that dismal wilderness.

"And, with a shudder, I thought it was creeping along,
Moving hundreds of limbs at once,

It wanted to grab me – in a terrifying frenzy
I let go of the coral's clinging branch;
At once the whirlpool seized me with raging force,
But it was my salvation, pulling me upwards."

At this the king is greatly amazed,
And says: "The goblet is yours,
And the ring, too, I will give you,
Adorned with the most precious stone
If you try once more, and bring me news
Of what you have seen on the sea's deepest bed."

His daughter hears this with tenderness,
And implores with coaxing words:
"Father, let the cruel game cease!
He has endured for you what no other can endure,
And if you cannot tame the desires of your heart,
then let the knights put the squire to shame."

Thereupon the king quickly seizes the goblet,
And hurls it into the whirlpool:
"If you return the goblet to this spot,
You shall be my noblest knight,
And you shall embrace as a bride this very day
The one who now pleads for you with tender pity."

Now his soul is seized with heavenly power,
And his eyes flash boldly,
And he sees the fair creature blush,
Then grow pale and swoon –
This impels him to gain the precious prize,
And he plunges down, to life or death.

The foaming waves are heard, they return,
Heralded by the thunderous roar –
She leans over with loving gaze:
The waves keep on returning,
Surging, they rise and fall;
Yet not one will bring back the youth.

(Translation from: Richard Wigmore, *Schubert: The Complete Song Texts* [New York, 1988], 122–126)

Shepherd's Lament (D121)

High on than mountain,
I have stood a thousand times,
Leaning on my staff,
And gazing down into the valley.

Then I follow the grazing flock,
Which my dog watches over for me.
I have come so low
And yet do not know how.

There stands the meadow
Full of beautiful flowers.
I pick them without knowing
Whom to give them to.

And rain, storm and thunder
I wait out underneath the tree.
The door there remains closed;
For all, alas, is but a dream.

There is a rainbow
Above that house!
But she has gone away,
Far away to distant lands.

To distant lands and farther,
Perhaps even over the sea.
Pass by, sheep, pass by!
Your shepherd's heart is aching.

Reichardt, "Dort droben in jenem Thale"

Over there in that valley
The water turns the wheel;
It turns nothing but love,
From evening until day.

The millwheel is broken
Love still has no end
If two people part from each other
They give each other their hands.

Ah! parting, ah! parting
Whoever thought of parting,
It has brought my young fresh life
To destruction.

There is no apple so beautiful, so round
That does not have two pips within,
There is no girl in the land
That does not have a false heart.

Who can trust them?
As soon as they're out of his sight,
A false heart and a haughty spirit
Is the way of all maidens.

Appendix

There in my father's garden
Stand two little trees
One bears nutmegs,
The other brown cloves.

Nutmegs are sweet,
Brown cloves smell so good
I want to give them to my darling
So that she may smell them.

The Miller's Farewell

High on that mountain
There stands a golden house,
Out from which every morning
Gaze three beautiful young maidens.

One is called Elisabeth
The other dear Bernharda,
The third, whom I will not name,
Should be my very own.

Down in that valley
The water turns a wheel
Which turns nothing but love
From evening until daytime again.

The wheel is broken,
Love has an end,
And when two lovers part,
They hold out their hands to one another.

Oh, parting, oh, oh!
Whoever invented parting
Made my innocent young heart
Already sorrowful.

This little song, oh, oh!
Was composed by a miller,
Whom the knight's daughter
Brought from love to parting.

The Young Nun (D828)

How the raging storm howls through the treetops!
The rafters clatter – the house trembles!
The thunder rolls – the lightning flashes! –
And the night is black as the tomb! –
    Still, still!

Appendix

So lately it raged also in me!
My life raged, as now the storm!
My limbs shook, as now the house!
My love flamed, as now the lightning,
And my heart was as black as the tomb! –

Now rage on, wild and mighty storm!
In my heart there is peace and tranquility!
The loving bride awaits the groom,
    Purified by the testing fire,
    Vowed to eternal love. –

I wait, my Savior, with longing eyes;
Come, heavenly bridegroom, claim your bride!
Free the soul from its earthly prison! –
Hark, the bell tolls peacefully from the tower;
Its sweet sound calls me all-powerfully to eternal heights –
    "Hallelujah!"

Pause (D795/12)

My lute I have hung on the wall,
And tied a green ribbon around it –
I cannot sing anymore, my heart is too full,
I don't know how to force it into rhyme.
The most ardent pangs of my longing
I once could express in playful song,
And as I lamented so sweetly and tenderly,
I thought that my suffering was not small.
Ah, how great is the burden of my happiness,
If no earthly music can contain it?

Now, dear lute, rest here on this nail!
And if a gentle breeze wafts across your strings,
Or if a bee brushes you with its wings,
Then I will feel fear and awe!
Why did I let the ribbon hang so far down?
Often it flutters against the strings with a sighing sound.
Is it the echo of my love's torment?
Shall it be the prelude to new songs?

NOTES

Introduction

1 *Allgemeine musikalische Zeitung* (hereafter *AmZ*), 26/26 (1824), 426: "Hr. Fr. S. schreibt keine eigentlichen Lieder und will keine schreiben . . . sondern freie Gesänge, manche so frei, dass man sie allenfalls Kapricen oder Phantasien nennen kann. Dieser Absicht gemäß sind die meist neuen Gedichte, deren Wert jedoch sehr verschieden ist, günstig gewählt und die Übertragung derselben in Töne im allgemeinen zu loben, da dem Verfasser fast durchaus die Anlage im ganzen und einzelnen, der Idee nach, aber bei weitem nicht so glücklich die Ausführung gelingt, die durch wenig oder gar nicht motiviertes exzentrisches, oft recht wildes Wesen und Treiben den Mangel innerer Einheit, Ordnung und Regelmäßigkeit zu ersetzen versucht; durch welche letzten Eigenschaften allein freilich kein Werk der Kunst zum schönen Kunstwerk wird, ohne welche Eigenschaften aber auch bestimmt nur bizarre, groteske Produkte entstehen." Otto Erich Deutsch tentatively identifies the author of this review as Gottfried Wilhelm Fink, editor of the *AmZ* from 1827 to 1841. (Unless otherwise indicated, the English translations in this study are my own.)

2 Otto Erich Deutsch, ed., *Schubert: Die Dokumente seines Lebens und Schaffens* (3 vols., Munich, 1914; enlarged edn., 1964, *Neue Ausgabe sämtliche Werke* (hereafter *NSA*), series viii, vol. V), 341: "Nur gestehe ich Ihnen offen, dass der eigne, sowohl oft geniale, also wohl auch mitunter etwas seltsame Gang Ihrer Geistesschöpfungen in unserem Publikum noch nicht genugsam und allgemein verstanden wird." The letter, dated August 26, 1826, is signed by the firm's agent, H. A. Probst.

3 *AmZ*, 30/4 (1828), 50: "greift er öfters, und zuweilen weit über die Gattung hinaus."

4 *AmZ*, 31/40 (1829), 656: "Eigentlicher Liedercomponist ist er nach unserm Dafürhalten nur zuweilen."

5 Concepts of voice and personae in art song are explored in Edward Cone's thought-provoking book *The Composer's Voice* (Berkeley and Los Angeles, 1974). (Cone's work was indeed one of the initial sources of inspiration for the present study.) There is a significant difference, however, between Cone's notion of the relation between drama and song and my own. Cone conceives every art song as a kind of miniature opera: "The poetic persona is transformed into what we have hitherto called the vocal persona: a character in a kind of monodramatic opera, who sings the original poem as his part" (p. 21). Cone does not differentiate among subcategories of Lieder. "Erlkönig" (D328) and "Der Tod und das Mädchen" (D531) are both described as mixed narrative-dramatic works, in

which a tension exists between the composer's persona (the "narrator," whose controlling hand is evident in the piano accompaniment, as well as in the melodic shape of the vocal line) and the characters represented.

In the present study, a somewhat different notion of "dramatic" is advanced. Songs which depict one or more specific personae engaged in a particular action, i.e., experiencing a change of circumstance, qualify as dramatic. This dramatic quality is reflected in both text and music. Songs which instead depict character *types* engaged in typical activities (e.g., a lover serenading his girl, or a mother rocking her child to sleep) do not fall into this category. These songs may generally best be described as lyrical. The fundamental thesis of this study, that Schubert transformed the Lied by combining elements of dramatic and lyrical genres, is based on the recognition of different subcategories of song.

6 Frankfurt *Allgemeiner musikalischer Anzeiger* (July 8, 1826): "Die musikalische Darstellung streift zuweilen, vielleicht nur ein wenig zu viel, ins Gebiet des Dramatischen, für welches uns Herr Schubert ganz besonders zu incliniren scheint."

7 *AmZ*, 31/40 (1829), 656: "wie vielen Völkern und Kämpfern, die mit dem Schwerte der Gewalt friedliche Gefilde bezwingen, von den Bezwungenen aber Bildung und Sprache annehmen."

8 Frankfurt *Allgemeiner musikalischer Anzeiger* 33 (1827), 318: "Diese Art Gesänge ist zu künstlich für das echte deutsche Lied und zu einfach, als daß man sie dramatisch nennen könnte."

9 Some valuable studies that touch on the subject of Schubert's dramatic songs are: Ludwig Scheibler, "Franz Schuberts einstimmige Lieder, Gesänge und Balladen mit Texten von Schiller," *Die Rheinlande* (April–Sept. 1905); Moritz Bauer, *Die Lieder Franz Schuberts* (Leipzig, 1915); Hermann Freiherr von der Pfordten, "Dramatische Deklamation bei Schubert," *Die Stimme*, 14 (1919–20), 195–204; Paul Mies, *Schubert, der Meister des Liedes* (Berlin, 1928); Hans Bosch, *Die Entwicklung des Romantischen in Schuberts Liedern* (Leipzig, 1930); Edith Schnapper, *Die Gesänge des jungen Schubert vor dem Durchbruch des romantischen Liedprinzips*, Berner Veröffentlichungen zur Musikforschung, vol. X (Bern and Leipzig, 1937); Joachim Kramarz, "Das Rezitativ im Liedschaffen Franz Schuberts" (Ph.D. diss., Free University of Berlin, 1959); Jürgen Mainka, "Das Liedschaffen Franz Schuberts in den Jahren 1815 und 1816: Schuberts Auseinandersetzung mit der Liedtradition des 18. Jahrhunderts (Ph.D. diss., Humboldt University, Berlin, 1958); Heinrich W. Schwab, *Sangbarkeit, Popularität und Kunstlied: Studien zu Lied und Liedästhetik der mittleren Goethezeit, 1770–1814,* Studien zur Musikgeschichte des neunzehnten Jahrhunderts, vol. III (Regensburg, 1965); Walter Wiora, *Das deutsche Lied: Zur Geschichte und Aesthetik einer musikalischen Gattung* (Wolfenbüttel and Zurich, 1971); John Reed, *The Schubert Song Companion* (Manchester, 1985).

10 The songs discussed in the *AmZ* review include "Auf der Donau" (D553), "Der Schiffer" (D536), "Wie Ulfru fischt" (D525), "Der Zwerg" (D771), "Wehmut" (D772), "Die Liebe hat gelogen" (D751), "Selige Welt" (D743), "Schwanengesang" (D744), "Schatzgräbers Begehr" (D761), "Gruppe aus dem Tartarus" (D583), and "Schlaflied" (D527). Those which depart significantly from the conventions of traditional Lieder are D553, D536, D771, D772, D761, and D583.

11 D583 was not Schubert's first attempt at setting Schiller's text. On May 11, 1813, while still a student at the Vienna Stadtkonvikt, he sketched a vocal canon

(D65) based on three lines from the poem ("Schmerz verzerret / Ihr Gesicht, Verzweiflung sperret / Ihren Rachen fluchend auf.") (The vocal canon, written for two tenors and bass, appears in vol. IV of the *NSA*, 180.) Then, in March 1816, he composed a solo setting of the full text (D396), of which only fourteen measures remain. (This fragmentary version appears in vol. II of the *NSA*, 171.) Whether Schubert abandoned the setting or the manuscript was simply mutilated is uncertain. In any case, this first solo setting bears only a slight resemblance to the later one and will not be discussed here.

12 The poem, composed around 1781, was first published in Schiller's *Anthologie auf das Jahr 1782*. Its subject corresponds to lines 540–627 of Virgil's epic. (*The Aeneid of Virgil*, verse trans. by Allen Mandelbaum [New York, 1971], 150–153.) Virgil's Tartarus episode (which echoes earlier passages in the Homeric epics) is, of course, also the chief classical source of Dante's *Inferno*. Dante's Christianized retelling of the classical episode, expanded to thirty-four cantos, recasts Aeneas and the Sibyl as the fictional Dante and Virgil. Here the classical poet guides the medieval man on his imaginary journey down into hell. While Schiller certainly knew of Dante's famous work, his poem makes no reference to Christian symbolism. The several classical allusions, including both "Tartarus" and "Cocytus," suggest that Virgil's text represented Schiller's primary source.

13 Johannes Brahms, for one, apparently thought the piano accompaniment had an orchestral quality. Sometime before 1871, he arranged Schubert's "Gruppe aus dem Tartarus" for one-part male chorus (tenors and basses in unison) and full orchestra.

14 *AmZ*, 26/26 (1824), 427: "Op. 24, No. 1 malt im Anfange, aber sehr gut, und die, obgleich sehr grellen, Modulationen lassen sich *hier* entschuldigen, allenfalls sogar rechtfertigen."

15 Schubert wrote two versions of this song. One, notated in 2/2 meter, is preserved in a fair copy with the title "Abendlied." The other, notated in 12/8, was the one published in October 1823 by Sauer and Leidesdorf as Op. 24, no. 2. In the Peters edition, this second version appears with the title "Schlummerlied."

16 Heinrich Christoph Koch, *Musikalisches Lexikon* (Frankfurt and Offenbach, 1802; reprint, 1964; abridged 1807 as *Kurzgefaßtes Handwörterbuch*), 901–904: "Lied. Mit diesem Namen bezeichnet man überhaupt jedes lyrische Gedicht von mehrern Strophen, welches zum Gesange bestimmt, und mit einer solchen Melodie verbunden ist, die bey jeder Strophe wiederholt wird, und die zugleich die Eigenschaft hat, dass sie von jedem Menschen, der gesunde und nicht ganz unbiegsame Gesangorgane besitzt, ohne Rücksicht auf künstliche Ausbildung derselben, vorgetragen werden kann. Hieraus folgt, dass die Melodie eines Liedes weder einen so weiten Umfang der Töne, noch solche Singmanieren und Sylbendehnungen enthalten darf, wodurch sich bloß der künstliche und ausgebildete Gesang der Arie auszeichnet, sondern daß der Ausdruck der in dem Texte enthaltenen Empfindung durch einfache, aber desto treffendere Mittel erlangt werden muß."

17 These characteristics are discussed at length in: Schwab, *Sangbarkeit, Popularität und Kunstlied*. See also: Wiora, *Das deutsche Lied*.

18 Other Schubert lullabies with many of the same characteristics include "Nachtgesang" (D119), "Wiegenlied" (D304), "An den Schlaf" (D447), "Wiegenlied" (D498), "Der Knabe in der Wiege" (D579), "Des Baches Wiegenlied" (D795/20), and "Wiegenlied" (D867).

19 Goethe is reported once to have said, "Ich kann nicht begreifen, wie Beethoven und Spohr das Lied [Mignon's "Sehnsucht"] so gänzlich mißverstehen konnten, als sie es durchkomponierten; die in jeder Strophe auf derselben Stelle vorkommenden Unterscheidungszeichen wären, sollte ich glauben, für den Tondichter hinreichend, ihn anzuzeigen, daß ich von ihm bloß ein Lied erwarte" (*Goethes Gespräche*, ed. F. von Biedermann, vol. II [Leipzig, 1909–11], 592).

20 The textual repeat in the last line of each stanza gives rise to 2+1-measure phrases at the end of the musical strophe, but this does not destroy the overall effect of regularity.

21 Two Schubert Lieder that have passed into the oral tradition are "Das Wandern" (D795/1) and "Der Lindenbaum" (D911/5, the first strophe only).

22 *AmZ*, 10/13 (1807), 194: "Die Vermischung verschiedener Gattungen ist nicht blos eine Klippe, die man in den Künsten wohl vermeiden muß; sie ist vielmehr eine Sünde, die das echte Talent nie begeht."

23 Schwab, *Sangbarkeit, Popularität und Kunstlied*, 13: "Die Reinheit der Gattung wird also zur eigentlichen Maxime."

24 *AmZ*, 34/24 (1832), 394: "Wenn gleichwohl Zelter's Lieder nicht überall verbreitet, nicht überall nach Würden geschätzt sind: so liegt das wohl nur daran, daß eben sehr Viele nicht mehr wissen oder nicht mehr beachten, was ein wahrhaft deutsches Lied ist und seyn soll; daß sie gewohnt worden sind, alle Gattungen des Gesanges durcheinander zu werfen . . ." The author of these lines is Friedrich Rochlitz, editor of the *AmZ* from 1798 to 1818.

25 As mentioned above, Fink probably wrote the critical review of Schubert's songs quoted at the beginning of this Introduction.

26 *AmZ*, 31/40 (1829), 655: "[N]atürlich und wahr ist es, daß da, wo man mit dem Bestande der Dinge nicht mehr zufrieden zu seyn geneigt ist, im Aufruhr alle Grenzen verrückt werden, wobey freylich auch manches Gute dahin stirbt, dessen Heimgang der unbefangene Beschauer zu beklagen sich genöthiget fühlt. Dass hingegen das Recht der Klage nur so lange auf seiner Seite seyn wird, so lange er in seiner Trauer sich nicht bis zum Ersterben aller Hoffnung eines neuen schönern Lenzes verleiten läßt, und so lange er das wohlthätig Reinigende den zuweilen höchst nothwendigen Stürmen nicht einseitig und kränklich matt abspricht, darf dabey keinesweges unberührt bleiben. – So ist es nun in unseren Tagen auch der Tonkunst ergangen. Manches sonst blühende Gebiet derselben hat seine Begrenzung eingebüßt. . . Namentlich hat dieses Schicksal jetzt jene mütterlich liebende Fürstin des Gesanges und vorzüglich die milde Beherrscherin des fruchtbaren Liederreiches erfahren."

27 *Ibid.*, 655: "Da er schon in seinen größeren Gesängen eine dem Dramatischen nahe stehende Eigenthümlichkeit offenbar genug beurkundet."

28 Zumsteeg's influence on Schubert and the relation between their settings of the same texts are treated at length in: Gunter Maier, *Die Lieder Johann Rudolf Zumsteegs und ihr Verhältnis zu Schubert* (Göppingen, 1971). Both Schubert's and Zumsteeg's settings of "Hagars Klage" appear in series iv, vol. VI of the *NSA*.

29 In some contexts, the term "mixed-genre Lieder" might usefully be applied to songs that combine characteristic traits of any two (or more) vocal traditions, e.g., lullaby and hymn. In this study, the term has a narrower application. It refers to songs that involve admixtures of poetic and musical traits from specifically *dramatic* vocal genres.

1 Neighboring genres and dramatic scenes before Schubert

1 The list on p. 18 is not intended as a complete or final catalogue of Schubert's dramatic scenes. Such a list would be impossible to create. While some songs clearly belong to this category, others are ambiguous. From one perspective they may seem to belong to the genre, from another not. Genres should be understood as groupings of works that share various traits, not rigid classification systems.

2 See Siegfried Goslich, "Die durchkomponierte Szene," in *Die deutsche romantische Oper* (Tutzing, 1975), 423–437; Winton Dean, "Italian Opera" and "German Opera," in *The Age of Beethoven 1790–1830*, ed. Gerald Abraham (London, 1982), 376–511, vol. VIII of *The New Oxford History of Music*.

3 See Paul Hamburger, "The Concert Arias," in *The Mozart Companion*, ed. H. C. Robbins Landon and Donald Mitchell (London, 1956), 324–360; Stefan Kunze, Introduction to *Bühnenwerke: Arien, Szenen, Ensembles und Chöre mit Orchester*, series ii, workgroup VII of *W. A. Mozart: Neue Ausgabe sämtliche Werke*, ed. Ernst Fritz Schmid, Wolfgang Plath, and Wolfgang Rehm (Kassel, 1955–).

4 The practice of performing operatic numbers in concert version did meet with criticism. An anonymous article published in the Leipzig *AmZ* during the spring of 1799 (1/31, 481–487) sharply denounces the custom. The author argues that extracting a scene from an opera is as nonsensical as extracting a scene from a play: it is impossible for the audience to understand and appreciate an operatic number outside its original dramatic context. Some concert directors, the author acknowledges, present only scenes which are relatively self-sufficient, depicting little or no action. Yet this restriction of subject, he argues, leads to routine forms: "Aber dafür entstehet auch hier das Uebel, daß solche Scenen so allgemein, so uninteressant, so unwirksam, und überdies einander selbst so ähnlich – oder vielmehr so ganz gleich sind, wie ein Strohhalm dem andern. Ein Eingang – so feyerlich, als ob, wer weiß was kommen sollte; ein Recitativ, mit vielen und leider gewöhnlich nur allzulangen Unterbrechungen des Gesanges, voll Seufzer und auf einmal wieder voll Toben; eine Arie, deren erster Theil in Zärtlichkeit schmilzt und die Herzen der Zuhorer schmelzen soll (zwischendurch marschmäßige Solosätzchen für Hörner und Hoboen thun nichts zur Sache); dann eine gewaltige Fermate, und nun ein hüpfendes oder wüthendes Allegro. Damit hat die Herrlichkeit ein Ende. Man könnte dies ein Recept für solche Kompositionen nennen. Man vergleiche zwanzig, dreysig und mehr dergleichen Scenen aus den neuesten deutschen und italienischen Opern, und überall ists dasselbe."

5 See Wolfgang Amadeus Mozart, *Briefe und Aufzeichnungen*, ed. Wilhelm A. Bauer and Otto Erich Deutsch (7 vols., Kassel, 1962). See also Mozart, *Verzeichnis aller meiner Werke* and Leopold Mozart, *Verzeichnis der Jugendwerke W. A. Mozarts*, ed. E. H. Mueller von Asow (Vienna and Wiesbaden, 1956).

6 Interestingly, although in Metastasio's play the aria belongs to a woman (the character Athalia), Schubert composed the song for a bass voice. The song was likely written for the singer Luigi Lablache, to whom the three Italian settings of Op. 83 were dedicated. This change of gender supports the notion that the audience's primary focus was on the singer, rather than the unnamed traitor in the text.

7 The most comprehensive study of the secular solo cantata in the eighteenth century is Eugen Schmitz's now somewhat outdated *Geschichte der Kantate und des geistlichen Konzerts. I. Teil: Geschichte der weltlichen Solokantate* (Leipzig, 1914).

8 Of course, not all secular solo cantatas of the late eighteenth and early nineteenth centuries were dramatic in nature, i.e., monologues or dialogues sung by identifiable characters. Composers also wrote occasional cantatas to celebrate events such as birthdays, namedays, and weddings. Schubert composed several such works, e.g., "Zur Namensfeier des Herrn Andreas Siller" (D83).

9 Several valuable studies of melodrama include Edgar Istel, *Die Entstehung des deutschen Melodramas* (Berlin and Leipzig, 1906); Hans Schauer and Friedrich Wilhelm Wodtke, "Monodrama," in *Reallexikon der deutschen Literaturgeschichte*, vol. II, 415–418 (Berlin, 1965); Kirsten Gram Holmström, *Monodrama, Attitudes, Tableaux Vivants: Studies of Some Trends of Theatrical Fashion 1770–1815* (Stockholm, 1967); Sybille Demmer, *Untersuchungen zu Form und Geschichte des Monodramas* (Cologne and Vienna, 1982).

10 *AmZ*, 1/7 (1798), 107–108.

11 *AmZ*, 1/25 (1799), 399–400.

12 "Ganymed" (D544) and "Prometheus" (D674), for example, show striking similarities to settings of the same texts by Reichardt. "Hagars Klage" (D5), "Die Erwartung" (D159), and the ballad "Ritter Toggenburg" (D397) were modeled after settings by Zumsteeg.

13 Herbing's vocal works are discussed in Max Friedländer, *Das deutsche Lied im 18. Jahrhundert: Quellen und Studien* (2 vols., Stuttgart and Berlin, 1902; reprint, 1970), vol. I, part 1, 142–146. See also Hermann Kretzschmar, *Geschichte des neuen deutschen Liedes*, part 1, Kleine Handbücher der Musikgeschichte nach Gattungen, vol. IV, 227–230 and 256–259.

14 Sack's dramatic songs are discussed in Friedländer, *Das deutsche Lied im 18. Jahrhundert*, vol. I, part 1, 160–161.

15 On the Lieder of the major Viennese composers, see Hans Boettcher, *Beethoven als Liederkomponist* (Augsburg, 1928); Ernst Bücken, "Die Lieder Beethovens: Eine stilkritische Studie," *Neues Beethoven Jahrbuch*, 2 (1925), 33–42; Maurice J. E. Brown, "Mozart's Songs for Voice and Piano," *The Music Review*, 17 (1956), 19–28; Hans Joachim Moser, "Mozart als Liederkomponist," *Österreichische Musikzeitschrift*, 11 (1956), 90–94; Gertraud Ebers, "Das Lied bei Haydn" (Ph.D. diss., University of Innsbruck, 1943).

16 See Walther Pauli, *Johann Friedrich Reichardt: Sein Leben und seine Stellung in der Geschichte des deutschen Liedes*, Musikwissenschaftliche Studien, vol. II (Berlin, 1903); Franz Flössner, *Reichardt, der Hallische Komponist der Goethezeit* (Halle, 1929); Walter Salmen, *Johann Friedrich Reichardt* (Freiburg, 1963).

17 Reprinted in *Das Erbe deutscher Musik*, ed. Walter Salmen, vols. LVIII–LIX (Munich–Duisburg, 1964).

18 Johann Friedrich Reichardt, *Vertraute Briefe, geschrieben auf einer Reise nach Wien und den österreichischen Staaten zu Ende des Jahres 1808 und zu Anfang 1809* (2 vols., Munich, 1915), vol. II, 48–49: "Bei all diesem eignen Kunsttreiben hab' ich gestern und ehegestern noch einigen öffentlichen Veranstaltungen mit Vergnügen beigewohnt. Madame Hendel gab mit ihrem Begleiter, der sich Patrick Peale nennt, das lang erwartete Deklamatorium im kleinen Redoutensaal, der mit einem ungewöhnlich glänzenden Publikum angefüllt war. Ihre Art zu

deklamieren kennst du. Herr Peale hat mir sehr gefallen, und ganz besonders im erzählenden Ton, in welchem er sehr fein das zarte Mittel zwischen malerischer Darstellung und trockner Erzählung hält. Auch in seinen ihm eignen Versuchen, die Deklamation mit Akkorden auf dem Fortepiano zu begleiten, und die Modulationen der Stimme den harmonischen Modulationen der Begleitung anzuzeigen und mit ihr zu verschmelzen, hab' ich mehr gefunden, als ich erwartete. Meine Begriffe von der gänzlichen Verschiedenheit der Natur der Rede und der des Gesanges sind dadurch erschüttert, und ich selbst bin auf neue Betrachtungen geleitet worden. Indes war auch bei dem neuen Versuche nicht zu verkennen, dass die absichtliche Bemühung, die Deklamation dem Gesange anzunähern, ohne daß sie doch selbst zu Gesang werde, etwas Eintöniges und Singendes in die Deklamation brachte, welches sich zu dem widerlichen Jammern und Winseln hinneigte, welches uns in früherer Zeit Ramlers übertriebener Deklamation so zuwider war."

19 Reichardt himself alludes to previous performances of poetic declamations.

20 Albert Stadler's collection, dated 1815, is housed in the Universitätsbibliothek Lund, Sammlung Taussig. The four Lieder by Reichardt appearing in vol. I of the collection comprise "Lied der Nacht," "Romanze" ["Kam ein Wandrer einst gegangen"], "Des Mädchens Klage," and "Rastlose Liebe."

21 See Hans Joachim Moser, "Carl Friedrich Zelter und das Lied," *Jahrbuch der Musikbibliothek Peters*, 39 (1932), 43–54; Gertraud Wittmann, *Das klavierbegleitete Sololied Karl Friedrich Zelters* (Giessen, 1936); Raymond Barr, "Carl Friedrich Zelter: A Study of the Lied in Berlin during the Late 18th and Early 19th Centuries" (Ph.D. diss., University of Wisconsin, 1968).

22 *Sämtliche Lieder, Balladen und Romanzen für das Pianoforte* (4 vols., Berlin, 1810–13; reprint, Hildesheim, Zürich, and New York, 1984).

23 See Ludwig Landshoff, *Johann Rudolph Zumsteeg (1760–1802): Ein Beitrag zur Geschichte des Liedes und der Ballade* (Berlin, 1902); Adolf Sandberger, "Johann Rudolph Zumsteeg und Franz Schubert," in *Ausgewählte Aufsätze zur Musikgeschichte* (Munich, 1921), 288–299; Franz Szymichowski, "Johann Rudolph Zumsteeg als Komponist von Balladen und Monodien" (Ph.D. diss., University of Frankfurt, 1932); Ernest G. Porter, "Zumsteeg's Songs," *The Monthly Musical Record*, 88 (1958), 135–40; Gunter Maier, *Die Lieder Johann Rudolf Zumsteegs und ihr Verhältnis zu Schubert* (Göppingen, 1971).

24 Johann Rudolf Zumsteeg, *Kleine Balladen und Lieder*, 7 vols. (Leipzig, 1800–05; facsimile edn., 1969).

25 *AmZ*, 13/2 (1811), 27–28: "Monolog der Thekla a.d. *Piccolomini*, als großes Declamations-Stück, wie man deren Hrn. R. schon mehrere verdankt, und worin man überall den meisterhaften Declamator und gebildeten, empfindungsvollen Mann, oftmals zugleich den mit Glück kühnen und tief greifenden Künstler erkennt. Sagt irgend eine Form den Eigenheiten des Hrn. R., als Musiker, vollkommen zu, so ist es diese."

26 A number of favorable reviews of Reichardt's "Deklamationen" appear in vols. 12 and 13 of the *AmZ*, dating from 1809–11.

27 This attitude is expressed, for example, in a review of Heinrich Karl Ebell's setting of Thekla's monologue from Schiller's *Wallensteins Tod* (*AmZ*, 3/26 [1801], 446): "Ich gestehe, daß dies kleine Werkchen die erste musikalische Komposition ist, welche mir von diesem Verf. bekannt worden, und daß ich sie mit

nichts weniger als günstigem Vorurtheil zur Hand genommen habe. Und in der That, einen Monolog, der nicht etwas wie Hamlets Seyn oder Nichtseyn auch außer seinem Zusammenhange verstanden und genossen werden kann; einen Monolog, der nichts Allgemeines hat, als Eine sehr schöne Sentenz, der voller historischen Details und Beziehungen ist und mit dem Ganzen des Stücks in unzertrennlicher Verbindung stehet – diesen herauszureißen und als ein Einzelnes in Musik gesezt herauszugeben, ist keinesweges ein glücklicher Gedanke."

28 *AmZ*, 5/20 (1803), 337: "[D]enn welcher Deutsche, der nur einigen Sinn für Poesie hat, hat sich nicht mit Schillers Jungfrau, und besonders auch mit diesem ihren vortrefflichen Monolog befreundet?" The writer continues, "Soll nun ein solches Stück einzeln in Musik gesezt werden, so vergreifen es wohl die Komponisten am allermeisten, die es, wie bey diesem und ähnlichen geschehen, des äußern Zuschnitts wegen, als Lied nehmen. Das hat Hr. S. nicht gethan, sondern es als freye, dramatische Scene gehandelt, und als solche, wie schon gesagt, recht sehr gut."

29 *Ibid.*, 336: "Die Italiener machen es allerdings oft so, besonders mit Scenen aus Metastasio; und wir fühlen uns beym Anhören solcher einzelnen Scenen weniger befremdet . . . [T]heils stehen viele der Metastasioischen Monologen und großen Solo-Scenen schon so einzeln und für sich (gut oder schlecht) bestehend im Gedicht, daß man sie auch einzeln, ohne etwas zu vermissen, aufnehmen kann; theils, und hauptsächlich, behandeln die Komponisten dann die nicht selten unbedeutenden Worte nur so obenhin, nur dem Allgemeinen des Sinnes nach und stellen die Musik so frey und selbsständig (ebenfalls gut oder schlecht) auf, daß man auf die Worte beym Anhören wenig oder gar nicht achtet."

2 Two contrasting examples of Schubert's dramatic scenes

1 Lines 3776–3833.

2 Schubert presumably used the first published edition of the play: *Faust. Eine Tragödie von Goethe* (Tübingen, 1808) (Maximilian and Lilly Schochow, eds., *Franz Schubert: Die Texte seiner einstimmig komponierten Lieder und ihre Dichter* [Hildesheim and New York, 1974]). Significantly, Schubert's setting of Gretchen's monologue from scene xv, "Gretchen am Spinnrade" (D118), dates from just two months earlier.

3 (a) Fair copy with the title "Aus Göthe's Faust." Also bears the heading: "Dom./ Amt. Orgel und Gesang./Gretchen unter vielem Volke. Böser Geist." Dated December 1814: Bibl. Nat., Paris, Sgl. Conservatoire, Ms. 270 [PhA 1044]; (b) Fair copy with the same title and heading. Also marked with the phrase "Skizze zu einer weitern Ausführung." Undated: Deutsche Staatsbibl., Berlin, Mus. Ms. autogr. Schubert 9.

4 In the *NSA*, the first version of the song appears written on three staves. In the "Quellen und Lesarten," however, Walther Dürr notes that the copy of the first version now housed in the Bibliothèque Nationale of Paris (which likely predated the other copy) is, with the exception of mm. 16–23, written on two staves.

5 For example, Walther Dürr, in the foreword to the *NSA*, states: "Die erste Fassung ist offenbar als dramatische Szene für Sopran- und Altsolo, Chor und Pianoforte gedacht. Hinweise wie *Tromboni* lassen den ursprünglichen Plan einer Orchesterbearbeitung erkennen – in den beiden erhaltenen autographen Rein-

schriften hat sich Schubert jedoch offensichtlich schon für das Klavier entschieden" (series iv: Lieder, vol. VII, xiv–xv). See also: Marius Flothuis, "Schubert revises Schubert," in *Schubert Studies: Problems of Style and Chronology*, ed. Eva Badura-Skoda and Peter Branscombe (Cambridge, 1982), 64 ("In my opinion . . . he imagined a dramatic scena accompanied by an orchestra").

6 Louis Spohr's opera *Faust* was composed in 1813 but not produced until 1816. The libretto, written by the Viennese writer Joseph Carl Bernard, differs significantly in outline from Goethe's play.

7 Otto Erich Deutsch, ed., *Schubert: Die Dokumente seines Lebens und Schaffens* (3 vols., Munich, 1914; enlarged edn., 1964, *NSA*, series viii, vol. V), 83.

8 Schubert originally notated Antigone's part in treble clef and Oedipus' part in bass clef, suggesting performance as a duet. When, however, the song was published in August 1821 by Cappi and Diabelli, the vocal line appeared (presumably with Schubert's endorsement) in treble clef throughout. The song was dedicated to Johann Michael Vogl, who certainly must have performed the work as a solo.

9 Fair copy with the title "Aus Göthe's Faust" and also the heading "Dom. Amt, Orgel und Gesang." Dated at beginning and end December 12, 1814. Now missing, previously in the possession of Leo Liepmannssohn, Berlin, Auktionskat. 37, Nov. 4–5, 1907, No. 221.

10 Deutsch, ed., *Schubert: Die Dokumente seines Lebens*, 40–41.

11 The remainder of this analysis will focus on the second version of the song.

12 Descending chromatic lines were to become one of Schubert's favorite musical symbols for death. Another significant motive in this passage is that of the sixth chord (i.e., the broken chords of the accompaniment in mm. 15–18 and the full chord in m. 19). This motive, which opens the second (but not the first) version of the song and reappears in mm. 29–30 during Gretchen's first outburst, is associated with the loud blasts of the trombone (m. 46) and the call of Judgment Day.

13 Schubert omits the line in brackets. The three verses may be translated as follows: "The day of wrath, that day / Will dissolve the world in ashes, / [As prophesied by David and the Sybil.] // And so when the Judge takes His seat / Whatever is hidden shall be manifest, / Nothing will remain unavenged. // What then, shall I, wretch, say? / Whom shall I ask to plead for me, / When scarcely the righteous shall be safe?"

14 A detailed study of "Der Tod und das Mädchen," written by Christoph Wolff ("Schubert's 'Der Tod und das Mädchen': Analytical and Explanatory Notes on the Song D531 and the Quartet D810"), appears in *Schubert Studies*, ed. Badura-Skoda and Branscombe. Wolff brings many fine insights to both Claudius's poem and Schubert's musical setting. I will not attempt to duplicate Wolff's efforts here, but will instead focus on the dramatic characteristics of the song.

15 Wolff, "Schubert's 'Der Tod und das Mädchen,'" 145.

16 The subject of "Der Tod und das Mädchen" derives from folklore. The tradition of representing Death as a skeleton dates back to the Middle Ages. See Rudolf Helm, *Skelett- und Todesdarstellungen bis zum Auftreten der Totentänze* (Strassburg, 1928). The symbolic encounter of the young girl and Death is itself reminiscent of the plays and pantomimes of fairground theatre.

17 Claudius writes "Das Mädchen" and "Der Tod" above the first and second stanzas, respectively. Significantly, Schubert retains these markings in the musical manuscript.

18 Wolff, "Schubert's 'Der Tod und das Mädchen,'" 156: "Oracle speech belongs to the technical repertory of Greek tragedy, either as inception of dramatic developments or as conclusion of a dramatic climax. When the gods predict the inevitable – and this is frequently a death sentence – the solemn voice of the oracle pronounces the verdict in a liturgical recitation-tone." One notable example of the oracle style is the voice of the Commendatore (statue) in Act II of Mozart's *Don Giovanni*.

3 Poetic and musical traits of the dramatic scene

1 Of these traits, all but the fourth are fundamental to the genre and exemplified by nearly every work. Mise-en-scène, while closely associated with the other traits, often remains ambiguous. When, however, the physical location of the action is described, the dramatic immediacy of the scene becomes greatly enhanced. Thus, although sometimes unclear, mise-en-scène represents one of the most powerful signals for the dramatic scene.

2 The sources for Schubert's song texts, where known, are given in: Maximilian and Lilly Schochow, eds., *Franz Schubert: Die Texte seiner einstimmig komponierten Lieder und ihre Dichter* (Hildesheim and New York, 1974).

3 Schubert did not always take the texts from their original dramatic sources. For "Amalia" (D195), he used a shorter version of the text published in the 1810 collection of Schiller's poetic works.

4 According to Maximilian and Lilly Schochow, Schubert probably used an edition of Schiller's poems, such as: *Friedrich von Schillers sämtliche Werke* (Stuttgart and Tübingen, 1812, etc.). This edition is a reprinting of the edition from 1804.

5 The history of Goethe's "Prometheus" monologue is described in G. Mackworth-Young's "Goethe's 'Prometheus' and its settings by Schubert and Wolf," *Proceedings of the Royal Musical Association*, 78 (1951–52), 53–65. In 1773, Goethe began to compose a Prometheus drama, based on the creation myth. After completing two acts, he abandoned the work. The monologue, composed in the following year, apparently precedes the action of the drama, though it includes various direct quotations. Goethe published the monologue with other assorted poems in 1779. The manuscript of the original drama, on the other hand, disappeared shortly after 1775. In 1819, a copy of the work resurfaced in Berlin. This discovery prompted the now aged poet to remark, in a letter to Zelter of May 1820, "Rather wonderful that that Prometheus which I myself had abandoned and forgotten should turn up again just now. The well-known monologue which is included among my poems was to have opened the third act." Because of the quotations from the first two acts of the drama and the earlier time reference, it seems improbable that the monologue was actually intended to open the third act. It is more likely that it represents the summation of Goethe's ideas on the Prometheus legend and marks his final rejection of the dramatic project.

6 One might be inclined to add novels to this list, specifically Goethe's *Wilhelm Meisters Lehrjahre*. However, Schubert's songs with texts drawn from Goethe's novel – the various versions of "Nur wer die Sehnsucht kennt," "Kennst du das Land," "Wer sich der Einsamkeit ergibt," "So laßt mich scheinen," "Wer nie sein

Brot," and "An die Türen will ich schleichen" – are best described not as dramatic scenes, but as mixed-genre Lieder. (These songs are identified as Lieder within the novel, where they are ostensibly sung. Settings by Reichardt appeared in the 1795 edition of the novel.)

7 For an overview of poetic genres during the late eighteenth and early nineteenth centuries, see Paul Böckmann, *Formgeschichte der deutschen Dichtung* (2 vols., Hamburg, 1949), and Johannes Klein, *Geschichte der deutschen Lyrik: Von Luther bis zum Ausgang des zweiten Weltkrieges* (Wiesbaden, 1957). Discussion of poetic theory during this period appears in Irene Behrens, *Die Lehre von der Einteilung der Dichtkunst vornehmlich vom 16. bis 19. Jahrhundert: Studien zur Geschichte der poetischen Gattungen* (Halle, Saale, 1940), and Klaus R. Scherpe, *Gattungspoetik im 18. Jahrhundert: Historische Entwicklung von Gottschen bis Herder* (Stuttgart, 1968).

8 See, for example, Emil Staiger, *Grundbegriff der Poetik* (Zurich, 1946), and T. S. Eliot, "The Three Voices of Poetry," in *On Poetry and Poets* (New York, 1957), 96–112.

9 *Aristotle's Poetics*, trans. S. H. Butcher (New York, 1961), 49.

10 *Ibid.*, 53.

11 Among the dramatic scene texts with regular structural patterns, there is much variety. For example, while the majority of texts have four-line stanzas, some have six-, eight-, ten-, and even twelve-line stanzas. The number of stanzas ranges from two to nineteen. There is also much diversity in the number of stressed syllables per line. "Philoktet" (D540) has three stressed syllables per line; "Antigone und Oedip" (D542) has four; "Hektors Abschied" (D312) has five; and "Gretchens Bitte" (D564), in some instances, as many as six. Trochaic and iambic meter predominate, but dactylic meter is also occasionally used. The pattern of rhyme and accentuation at line endings varies from text to text.

12 There are some small structural irregularities. Line 21 ("Aber meine Liebe nicht"), for example, breaks from the prevailing pattern of five stressed syllables per line, granting additional force to the poetic sentiment.

13 The text is taken from James Macpherson's prose-poem *Carric-Thura*.

14 The scarcity of genre titles among Schubert's dramatic scenes seems all the more striking in comparison with other song types, where such titles abound: e.g., Wiegenlied, Grablied, Ständchen, Hymne, Fischerlied, Klaglied, Nachtlied, Morgenlied, Schwanengesang, Frühlingslied. These traditional genre headings call attention to the community of works with which a particular song is associated. One appreciates these works by identifying the *kinds* of song setting they represent, whether lullaby, funeral dirge, serenade, or hymn. Here, the question "who is speaking?" can be answered only in a most general way: a mother, mourner, lover, or chorister. And indeed, one does not need to know more. The titles of Schubert's dramatic scenes, by contrast, emphasize the uniqueness of character and dramatic situation. Drama replaces music as the primary focus of attention.

15 Gustav Schilling's definition of *Scene*, included in the *Encyclopädie der gesammten musikalischen Wissenschaften, oder Universal-Lexikon der Tonkunst* (Stuttgart, 1835–38), lends further support to a broad conception of the genre, embracing both monologue and dialogue texts: "Als gewißermassen Darstellung der Handlung selbst ist die Scene in der Musik ein Singstück oder Haupttheil eines

Singstücks von gewöhnlich streng recitativischer Haltung, worin der Text *in Form des Dialogs oder Monologs* irgend eine Handlung oder die Theilnahme an solcher ausspricht" (emphasis added).

16 The second half of m. 54 echoes the first half – the setting of the word "löste," which comes at the end of Gretchen's second statement. The echo suggests that, although representing inner thoughts, her words are spoken aloud (just as the evil spirit externalizes the voice of her conscience).

4 The dramatic ballad tradition

1 None of Schubert's dramatic ballads have texts consisting entirely of dialogue, but some strophic ballads do. One well-known example is "Eine altschottische Ballade" (D923).

2 Some of the dramatic ballads are not completely throughcomposed. These exceptions will be discussed later in the chapter.

3 See note 7 below.

4 Philipp Spitta, "Die Ballade," in *Musikgeschichtliche Aufsätze* (Berlin, 1894), 409: "[D]er lebhafte Wechsel der Empfindungen und Stimmungen, die Mannigfaltigkeit der Vorgänge, das Streben der Dichter nach greifbarster Bildlichkeit – alles dies musste den Musiker mahnen, dass auch seiner Kunst dergleichen darzustellen nicht unmöglich sei."

5 Of course, strophic ballads were not entirely forsaken. As noted, Schubert himself composed many such songs.

6 Heinrich Christoph Koch, *Musikalisches Lexikon* (Frankfurt and Offenbach, 1802; reprint, 1964; abridged 1807 as *Kurzgefaßte Handwörterbuch*), 212–213: "Die Melodie der Ballade, deren Charakter von dem Inhalte des Gedichts bestimmt wird, ist weder an eine besondere Form, noch an eine besondere Taktart gebunden. Seit einiger Zeit hat man angefangen, sie nicht so, wie bey dem Liede, mit jeder Strophe des Textes zu wiederholen, sondern den Text ganz durch zu komponieren."

7 *Ibid.*, 212: "Eine Art von Gesang über mehrere Strophen eines Gedichtes dessen Hauptinhalt Liebe ist, und die, weil sie ursprünglich tanzend gesungen wurde, einen dazu angemessenen Gang der Verse hatte. . . Unserer modernen Balladen weichen nicht merklich von den Romanzen ab, und erfordern, weil sie anjetzt blos zum Gesange bestimmt sind, eine lyrische Versart."

8 Koch, *Kurzgefaßtes Handwörterbuch*, 46: *Ballade* bezeichnet eine sehr bestimmte und charakteristische Dichtungsart. Sie ist eine Erzählung einer Begebenheit, die entweder abentheurlich, oder wunderbar, oder schauerlich, oder tragi-komisch, oder alles dies zu gleicher Zeit ist. Liebe ist dabey jederzeit im Spiele, ob es gleich nicht gerade eine Liebesbegebenheit zwischen unverheiratheten Personen seyn muss, welche erzählt wird.

Obgleich die Ballade kein lyrisches Gedicht ist, so ist sie dennoch zum Gesang bestimmt."

9 Max Friedländer, *Das deutsche Lied im 18. Jahrhundert: Quellen und Studien* (2 vols., Stuttgart and Berlin, 1902; reprint, 1970), vol. I, part 1, 215: "die erste durchcomponirte Ballade, die wir in der deutschen Musik besitzen." This and other

settings of "Lenore" appear in: *Balladen von Gottfried August Bürger, in Musik gesetzt von André, Kunzen, Zumsteeg, Tomaschek und Reichardt*, ed. Dietrich Manicke, vols. XLV–XLVI of *Das Erbe deutscher Musik* (Mainz, 1970).

10 For a full discussion of Zumsteeg's ballads, including "Lenore," see Franz Szymichowski, "Johann Rudolph Zumsteeg als Komponist von Balladen und Monodien" (Ph.D. diss., University of Frankfurt, 1932). Loewe himself had great respect for Zumsteeg's compositional talent, as indicated by this statement appearing in his autobiography: "Tief ergriff mich die Musik dieses alten, mit Unrecht zurückgestellten Meisters. Ihre Motive sind characteristisch und geistreich, sie folgen dem Gedichte mit vollkommener Treue. Freilich waren sie meist sehr aphoristischer Natur. Ich dachte mir, die Musik müßte dramatischer sein und unter breiter ausgearbeiteten Motiven gestaltet werden, etwa so, wie ich meine Balladen zu setzen versucht habe. Doch ist das Verdienst Zumsteegs als Balladen-Componist unbestritten" (Karl Loewe, *Selbstbiographie*, ed. Carl Hermann Bitter [Berlin, 1870], 70).

11 The first date indicates the time of composition; the second date shows when the work was first published.

12 Included in the volumes are also a selection of strophic ballads and romances. These songs are not dramatic and thus lie outside the scope of the present discussion.

13 At least five reviews of Zumsteeg's ballads appear in vols. 1–3 of the *AmZ*, published during 1799–1800. The *AmZ* also printed reviews of ballads by Reichardt (vol. 2) and Tomaschek (vol. 15), as well as articles on ballads generally (vols. 1 and 2). Other journals, such as the Berlin *Musikalische Wochenblatt*, the *Allgemeine Literatur Zeitung*, and Schubart's *Chronik*, contain additional reviews.

14 See Otto Erich Deutsch, ed., *Schubert: Die Erinnerungen seiner Freunde* (Leipzig, 1957, 3rd edn., 1974; Eng. trans. as *Schubert: Memoirs by his Friends*, London, 1958).

15 Deutsch, ed., *Schubert: Memoirs by his Friends*, 26–27.

16 *Ibid.*, 58.

17 *Ibid.*, 127. These remarks were written in 1858.

18 Gunter Maier, *Die Lieder Johann Rudolf Zumsteegs und ihr Verhältnis zu Schubert* (Göppingen, 1971).

5 An example of Schubert's dramatic ballads

1 The differences between the first and second versions of "Der Taucher" are discussed by Walther Dürr in *NSA*, series iv, volume VI, Vorwort, xvi–xviii. The present analysis will focus on the second version of the song.

2 See, in particular, the ballads of Ludwig Heinrich Christoph Hölty and Gottfried August Bürger.

3 "Und es wallet und siedet und brauset und zischt, / Wie wenn Wasser mit Feuer sich mengt, / Bis zum Himmel spritzet der dampfende Gischt. . ."

6 Poetic and musical traits of the dramatic ballad

1 The late eighteenth-century enthusiasm for folk poetry received its initial impetus from the publication in 1765 of Bishop Thomas Percy's *Reliques of Ancient English Poetry*. This collection of English and Scottish folk songs and ballads helped to thaw the haughty attitude toward folk art held by men of letters and sparked the imagination of poets and composers alike. Many collections of authentic folks songs and ballads appeared, most notably Johann Gottfried Herder's *Volkslieder* of 1778–79 and Achim von Arnim and Clemens Brentano's *Des Knaben Wunderhorn* of 1808. Johann Wolfgang Goethe, who also traveled through the countryside collecting Volkslieder, wrote a number of poems in a folk idiom, including "Heidenröslein," "Ein Veilchen auf der Wiese stand," "Der König von Thule," and (as discussed in Chapter 7) "Schäfers Klagelied."

2 In *The Rhetoric of Fiction* (Chicago and London, 1961), Wayne C. Booth states, "to say that a story is told in the first or the third person will tell us nothing of importance unless we become more precise and describe how the particular qualities of the narrators relate to specific effects" (p. 150). Although the narratives in Schubert's dramatic ballads are far less complex than the novels which form the focus of Booth's discussion, his ideas concerning dramatized and undramatized narrators are highly suggestive for these songs, as well as for certain mixed-genre Lieder. For instance, there is a fundamental difference between the "third person" narrators of "Die Bürgschaft" (D246) and "Die Forelle" (D550). In the first case, the narrator remains outside the events of the story, never once revealing his emotions. In the second, while the narrator again stands apart from the action (the fisherman's capturing of the fish), he is outraged by the treachery he witnesses and describes. By exposing his anger, the narrator of "Die Forelle" in effect becomes a character in his own story; "third person" merges with "first person." In most of Schubert's dramatic ballads, the narrative posture resembles that of "Die Bürgschaft."

3 Edward Cone discusses various interpretations of the narrator's role in Schubert's "Erlkönig" in *The Composer's Voice* (Berkeley and Los Angeles, 1974), 5–8.

4 None of Schubert's dramatic ballad texts comprise *only* dialogue, like the strophic ballad "Eine altschottische Ballade" (D923). Dramatic songs with wholly dialogue texts instead constitute dramatic scenes.

5 A smaller number have five, six, or seven lines. Only a few ballads have irregular stanzas of varying length.

6 The only exceptions are "Liedesend" (D473) with three stresses throughout, "Der Zwerg" (D771) with five stresses, and "Leichenfantasie" (D7) with an irregular number of stresses.

7 Just a few ballads have dactylic metrical schemes, either throughout, as in "Minona" (D152), or alternating with other metrical patterns, as in "Erlkönig" (D328), "Die Bürgschaft" (D246), and "Amphiaraos" (D166).

8 The moral at the end of "Der Vatermörder" (D10) is highly unusual: "Du, heiliges Gewissen, bist / Der Tugend letzter Freund; / Ein schreckliches Triumphlied ist / Dein Donner ihrem Feind."

9 Richard Capell, *Schubert's Songs* (London, 1928; reprint, 1957), 113.

10 In present-tense narratives, there is plainly a greater need for general correspondence between story time and narrative time.

11 This observation fits nicely with Edward Cone's notion that the piano accompaniment in an art song has a narrative function (*The Composer's Voice*, p. 12).

7 Lyrical songs with admixtures of dramatic traits

1 Not all modified strophic songs are usefully considered mixed-genre Lieder as defined in this study. In some cases, such as "Andenken" (D99), the variation principle appears to be essentially a musical phenomenon, and does not reflect dramatic action in the text.

2 The reception history of "Der Lindenbaum" (D911/5), with the similar form A A' B A", supports the notion of generic mixture. "Der Lindenbaum" has passed into the oral tradition, but with an important difference: it is sung as a purely strophic song. The dramatic contrast supplied by the B section, as well as the modal and accompanimental changes in the repetitions of the A section, are omitted.

3 The text of "Gretchen am Spinnrade," like that of "Szene aus Faust," constitutes an entire scene in Goethe's play. Unlike "Der König in Thule," the words are not intended to be sung on stage.

4 The lists of mixed-genre Lieder provided in Chapters 7, 8, and 9 represent a sampling of works that fit each category, not a complete catalogue. Instead of attempting to classify every mature Schubert song (an unworthy and probably impossible task), I have tried to identify a number of particularly good examples.

5 There are two versions of "Schäfers Klagelied." The first, dated November 30, 1814, is composed in c minor and has no piano introduction. A copy of this version was included in the collection of songs sent to Goethe in 1816. For the Jaell program, Schubert transposed the song to e minor and added a four-measure piano introduction. Aside from these changes, the two versions are nearly identical. This analysis will focus on the first version of the song.

6 The Berlin *Gesellschafter*, for example, stated: "Ein Gesangstück: 'Schäfers Klagelied,' von dem jungen Schubert komponiert und gesungen von unserem braven Tenoristen Jäger, gewährte den meisten Genuß. Man freut sich in der Tat recht sehr auf ein größeres, uns zum Genuß bevorstehendes Werk dieses hoffnungsvollen Künstlers" (Deutsch, ed., *Schubert: Die Dokumente seines Lebens und Schaffens* [3 vols., Munich, 1914; enlarged edn., 1964, *NSA*, series viii, vol. V], 78).

7 Otto Erich Deutsch, ed., *Schubert: Die Dokumente seines Lebens*, 126–130: "Hier ist alles vereint, um es zum vollendeten Tonwerke zu machen. Der dem Pastorale eigentümliche Ton ist vortrefflich gehalten: er liegt schon im melodischen Ausdrucke. Die Begleitung ist zweckmäßig und verbindet die durch die charakteristischen Modifikationen notwendig auseinander gehaltenen Melodien. Letztere sind schon an und für sich reizend und wirken als ästhetische Ideen auch ohne Text und Harmonie; jede Note muß unverrückt bleiben, soll die Melodie nicht zerstört werden, der sichere Probestein ihrer organischen Natur! Die Charakteristik ist so tief eingreifend, daß sie keiner Auseinandersetzung bedarf, um allgemein empfunden zu werden. Auch die Übergänge im charakteristischen Ausdrucke sind hier höchst natürlich und ergreifend!"

8 The text is given here as it appears in Schubert's song. Schubert made several small changes to Goethe's poem: (1) addition of "hin" in line 3, (2) "weg" changed to "fort" in line 19, (3) addition of "nur" in line 23, 4) repetition of the final two lines of stanza 6 ("Vorüber, ihr Schafe, nur vorüber! / Dem Schäfer ist gar so weh.")

9 Frederick W. Sternfeld, *Goethe and Music: A List of Parodies and Goethe's Relationship to Music* (New York, 1954), 9.

10 "Ich lege Dir auch eine kleine Romanze bei, die Goethe nach einer Volksmelodie, die er kürzlich hier singen hörte, und die vom Rheine kommt, gemacht hat." (Gerhard Graf, ed., *Goethe über seine Dichtungen*, Part III: *Die lyrischen Dichtungen*, vol. 1 [Frankfurt, 1912], 370).

11 Johann Friedrich Reichardt, *Musikalisches Kunstmagazin* (2 vols., Berlin, 1782–91; reprint, 1969), vol. I, 99.

12 *Ibid.*, "eine zweiten Stimme nach Waldhornart."

13 Achim von Arnim and Clemens Brentano, eds., *Des Knaben Wunderhorn* (3 vols., Heidelberg, 1806–08).

14 Ludwig Erk and Franz M. Böhme, *Deutscher Liederhort* (3 vols. Leipzig, 1893–94), vol. II, 234.

15 Zelter's simple strophic setting of "Schäfers Klagelied" dates from this year.

16 Sternfeld, *Goethe and Music*, 8–13.

17 Sternfeld, *Goethe and Music*, 8.

18 Goethe himself seems to invite such a comparison, for the opening line of his poem echoes that of the folk text.

19 Schubert's choice of meter, of course, has much to do with the stress pattern of Goethe's poetry which was itself composed to fit preexisting music, probably in $\frac{6}{8}$ time. The folk song variant published in Reichardt's *Musikalisches Kunstmagazin*, although marked with a $\frac{3}{4}$ time signature, is written in $\frac{3}{8}$ time.

20 Goethe's use of the perfect tense emphasizes the finality of this event.

8 Dramatic songs with admixtures of lyrical traits

1 According to legend, St. Agnes was martyred at the early age of thirteen. Because she refused to marry, her chastity was violated before her execution. Nevertheless, she miraculously remained a virgin. Superstition had it that on St. Agnes's Eve, if a young girl performed certain rites, she would see a vision of her future husband. Two famous poems based on this legend are Keats's "The Eve of St. Agnes" (1819) and Tennyson's "St. Agnes' Eve" (1833). In Tennyson's poem, as in Craigher's (1823), the young girl is a nun.

2 Interestingly, the diminished fifth motive (a seemingly "purified" version of the "evil" diminished fifth motive in the piano left hand at m. 22) appears in a similar dramatic context in another Craigher setting, dating from approximately the same period as "Die junge Nonne" (April 1825). In "Totengräbers Heimweh" (D842), the poetic persona is a grave-digger, weary with the burden of his profession and plagued by the meaninglessness of life. His extended monologue, like that of the young nun, expresses an intense desire for the eternal peacefulness of death – a wish that is eventually fulfilled. The moment of transition from life to death occurs at the line "Es schwinden die Sterne, – das Auge schon bricht" (mm. 63–66). To emphasize its meaning, Schubert sets this line with the unusual melodic gesture of a falling diminished fifth. Although the harmonic context differs from that in "Die junge Nonne," the falling diminished fifth motive is

again clearly associated with death. (Schubert stresses the association by repeating the motive six more times in the succeeding measures.) This motive is also associated with death in the ballad "Der Zwerg" (D771), where it appears in mm. 81–86 at the line "Doch mußt zum frühen Grab du nun erblasen."

3 The repetition, during which the nun reflects upon her previous emotional state, is actually slightly shorter than the original version. Here, the piano introduction and the beginning of the vocal part are condensed and superimposed on one another. Each statement of the principal melodic/rhythmic motive, alternating between the vocal part and the piano left hand, highlights a particular poetic image.

9 Lyrico-dramatic songs

1 John Reed, *The Schubert Song Companion* (Manchester, 1985), 425.

2 "Pause" has been the subject of many published analyses, including: Alfred Heuss, "Eine Schubert-Liedstudie: Das Lied 'Pause' aus dem Zyklus *Die schöne Müllerin,*" *Zeitschrift für Music,* 91 (1924), 617–626; Franz Valentin Damian, "Über das Lied 'Pause' aus Schuberts Liederkreis *Die schöne Müllerin,*" in *Schubert-Gabe der Oesterreichischen Gitarre-Zeitschrift* (Vienna, 1928), 35–43; Thrasybulos Georgiades, *Schubert: Musik und Lyrik* (Göttingen, 1967), 262–266; Arnold Feil, *Franz Schubert: "Die schöne Müllerin," "Winterreise"* (Stuttgart, 1975), 81–83; and Lawrence Kramer, "The Schubert Lied: Romantic Form and Romantic Consciousness," in *Schubert: Critical and Analytical Studies,* ed. Walter Frisch (Lincoln, NE and London, 1986), 215–218.

3 The miller's spirits do not explicitly begin to sink until two songs later, "Der Jäger." In the thirteenth song of the cycle, "Mit dem grünen Lautenbande," the miller is still reasonably cheerful. Note, however, the tempo indication "Mäßig."

4 Ann Clark Fehn and Rufus Hallmark, "Text and Music in Schubert's Pentameter Lieder: A Consideration of Declamation," in *Music and Language* (New York, 1983), 204–246.

5 Several small rhythmic changes are necessitated by the differing patterns of weak stresses within the individual lines.

6 Lowercase letters designate the musical setting of individual poetic lines. Uppercase letters represent large musical sections.

7 In both stanzas, the vocal part eventually loses its declamatory character and becomes more melodic (mm. 35–40 and mm. 66–69, 74–77).

8 This augmented sixth parallels the earlier one in mm. 39–40.

9 This interpretation raises several intriguing questions. Since the miller has presumably laid the instrument aside, why does Schubert compose "lute music" here? Who is playing it? Here it is important to recognize that the lute has assumed a quasi-independent existence, almost as if it were a separate character. Significantly, the keyboard music of this first section can hardly be said to "accompany" the vocal part. Rather, the two just happen to coincide. The absence of "harmony" between the two parts is suggested, for example, at the downbeat of m. 11: the vocal line calls for a dominant harmony, but the accompaniment presents the subdominant over a tonic pedal, resulting in a discordant clash.

10 Following the same principle of even declamation, the third poetic line, with four stresses, is two measures long.

11 Whether we are really to believe him, however, remains an open question. After all, this song, like the preceding ones, is in fact sung; it is not a melodrama. Indeed, in the very phrase that the miller disclaims his ability to sing (measures 15–16), the music momentarily becomes more active, more melodic; not only does the tonic pedal disappear, but the vocal line and piano's right hand move in counterpoint through undulating melodic arches. This music is certainly more melodious than anything yet heard (aside from the piano introduction). Similarly, just when the miller says he no longer knows how to rhyme, his verses do just that: "Ich kann nicht mehr singen, mein Herz ist zu *voll*, / Weiß nicht, wie ich's in Reime zwingen *soll*." Is the miller aware of the discrepancy between his words and their effect? Is he the unwitting victim of authorial mockery? At this point in the song, it is unclear.

12 Significantly, lines 5 and 7, both of which are set with the b1 music, do not have the same number of stressed syllables: line 5 has five stresses while line 7 has only four. Schubert nevertheless gives them the same number of measures, suggesting that he desired a balanced structural effect. In the A section, by contrast, line 3 (again with four stresses) has a shorter musical duration than the other lines.

13 Maximilian and Lilly Schochow, eds., *Franz Schubert: Die Texte seiner einstimmig komponierten Lieder und ihre Dichter* (Hildesheim and New York, 1974), 385.

14 The return of the tonic in m. 42 represents a new beginning, not a continuation.

15 From this perspective, the one-and-a-half-measure delay of the vocal entrance (mm. 56–57) takes on a special significance. The sound of the lute, represented by the accompanimental music, inspires the miller's response. He is drawn into this mysterious realm by a voice from afar. (Note that the passage is marked pianissimo).

16 The only other consecutive songs in the same key are "Des Müllers Blumen" and "Thränenregen."

17 Schubert emphasizes the tonal relation between the two songs by beginning "Mit dem grünen Lautenbande" with a sustained B♭ chord, which echoes the final cadence of "Pause." Although the chord is often viewed as extraneous and omitted in performance, it actually serves an important function in highlighting the connection between "Pause" and the following song.

18 The major mode resolution in the final bars of "Pause" foreshadows the dissolving of grief into blissful lyricism at the end of the song cycle.

BIBLIOGRAPHY

Pre-1850 titles

Allgemeine musikalische Zeitung, ed. Friedrich Rochlitz, Gottfried Wilhelm Fink, et al. Leipzig, 1798–1848.

Arnim, Achim von, and Clemens Brentano, eds. *Des Knaben Wunderhorn*. 3 vols. Heidelberg, 1806–08.

Avison, Charles. *An Essay on Musical Expression*. London, 1752.

Bach, Johann Ernst. *Sammlung auserlesener Fabeln*. Nuremberg, 1749.

Chabanon, Michel-Paul-Guy de. *Observations sur la musique et principalement sur la métaphysique de l'art*. Paris, 1779; ed. and trans. Johann Adam Hiller. Leipzig, 1781.

Engel, Johann Jakob. *Über die musikalische Malerei*. Berlin, 1780.

Herbing, Valentin. *Musicalischer Versuch in Fabeln und Erzählungen*. Leipzig, 1759.

Hiller, Johann Adam. *Anweisung zum musikalisch-richtigen Gesange*. Leipzig, 1774.

Anweisung zum musikalisch-zierlichen Gesange. Leipzig, 1780.

Koch, Heinrich Christoph. *Musikalisches Lexikon*. Frankfurt am Main and Offenbach, 1802. Reprint, 1964. Abridged 1807 as *Kurzgefaßtes Handwörterbuch*.

Krause, Christian Gottfried. *Von der musikalischen Poesie*. Berlin, 1752.

Krause, Christian Gottfried, and Carl Wilhelm Ramler, eds. *Oden mit Melodien*. 2 vols. Berlin, 1753, 1755.

Marpurg, Friedrich Wilhelm, ed. *Berlinische Oden und Lieder*. 3 vols. Berlin, 1756, 1759, 1763.

Historisch-Kritische Beyträge zur Aufnahme der Musik. 5 vols. Berlin, 1754–78.

Neefe, Christian Gottlob. *Serenaten beim Klavier zu Singen*. Leipzig, 1777.

Reichardt, Johann Friedrich. *Goethes Lieder, Oden, Balladen und Romanzen*. 4 vols. Leipzig, 1809–11. Reprint, *Das Erbe deutscher Musik*, ed. Walter Salmen, vols. LVIII–LIX. Munich, 1964.

Schillers lyrische Gedichte. 2 vols. Leipzig, 1810.

Vertraute Briefe, geschrieben auf einer Reise nach Wien und den österreichischen Staaten zu Ende des Jahres 1808 und zu Anfang 1809. 2 vols. Munich, 1915.

Reichardt, Johann Friedrich, ed. *Musikalisches Kunstmagazin*. Berlin, 1782–91. Reprint. 1969.

Rousseau, Jean Jacques. *Dictionnaire de Musique*. Paris, 1768.

Schilling, Gustav, ed. *Encyclopädie der gesammten musikalischen Wissenschaften, oder Universal-Lexikon der Tonkunst*. 6 vols. Stuttgart, 1835–38.

Bibliography

Schulz, Johann Abraham Peter. *Lieder im Volkston*. 3 vols. Berlin, 1782, 1785, 1790.

Sulzer, Johann Georg, ed. *Allgemeine Theorie der schönen Kunste*. Leipzig, 1771–74.

Zelter, Carl Friedrich. *Sämtliche Lieder, Balladen und Romanzen für das Pianoforte*. 4 vols. Berlin, 1810–13. Reprint. Hildesheim, Zurich, and New York, 1984.

Zumsteeg, Johann Rudolf. *Kleine Balladen und Lieder*. 7 vols. Leipzig, 1800–05. Facsimile edn. 1969.

Post-1850 Titles

Abert, Hermann. *Niccolo Jommelli als Opernkomponist*. Halle, 1908.

"Wort und Ton in der Musik des achtzehnten Jahrhunderts," *Archiv für Musikwissenschaft*, 5 (1923), 31–70.

Alberti-Radanowicz, Editha. "Das Wiener Lied von 1789–1815," *Studien zur Musikwissenschaft*, 10 (1923), 37–78.

Ambros, August Wilhelm. "J. R. Zumsteeg, der Balladencomponist," in *Bunte Blätter: Skizzen und Studien für Freunde und der bildenden Kunst*, new ser., 65–92. Leipzig, 1874.

Ansion, Margarete, and Irene Schlaffenberg, eds. *Das Wiener Lied von 1778 bis Mozarts Tod*. Denkmäler der Tonkunst in Österreich, issue 27/2, vol. LIV. Vienna, 1920.

Aristotle, *Aristotle's Poetics*, trans. S. H. Butcher. New York, 1961.

Bach, Johann Christian. *Johann Christian Bach: 12 Konzert- und Opern-Arien*, ed. Ludwig Landshoff. 1930.

Badura-Skoda, Eva, and Peter Branscombe, eds. *Schubert Studies: Problems of Style and Chronology*. Cambridge, 1982.

Barr, Raymond. "Carl Friedrich Zelter: A Study of the Lied during the Late 18th and Early 19th Centuries." Ph.D. diss., University of Wisconsin, 1968.

Bauer, Moritz. *Die Lieder Franz Schuberts*. Leipzig, 1915.

Beethoven, Ludwig van. *Ludwig van Beethovens Werke: Vollständige kritisch durchgesehene überall berechtigte Ausgabe*. Series xxii: *Gesänge mit Orchester*. Series xxiii: *Lieder und Gesänge*. Series xxv: Supplement: *Gesang-Musik*. Leipzig, 1864–90.

Behrens, Irene. *Die Lehre von der Einteilung der Dichtkunst vornehmlich vom 16. bis 19. Jahrhundert: Studien zur Geschichte der poetischen Gattungen*. Halle, Saale, 1940.

Bloch, Henry. "Tommaso Traetta's Contribution to the Reform of Italian Opera," in *Collectanea Historiae Musicae*, vol. III, 5–13. Florence, 1963.

Böckmann, Paul. *Formgeschichte der deutschen Dichtung*. 2 vols. Hamburg, 1949.

Boettcher, Hans. *Beethoven als Liederkomponist*. Augsburg, 1928.

Booth, Wayne C. *The Rhetoric of Fiction*. Chicago and London, 1961.

Bosch, Hans. *Die Entwicklung des Romantischen in Schuberts Liedern*. Leipzig, 1930.

Branscombe, Peter. "Schubert and the Melodrama," in *Schubert Studies: Problems of Style and Chronology*, ed. Eva Badura-Skoda and Peter Branscombe, 105–141. Cambridge, 1982.

Brown, Maurice J. E. "Mozart's Songs for Voice and Piano," *The Music Review*, 17 (1956), 19–28.

Schubert Songs. London, 1967.

Brown, Maurice J. E., and Eric Sams. "Schubert," *The New Grove Dictionary of Music and Musicians*, ed. Stanley Sadie. London, 1980.

Bibliography

Bücken, Ernst. *Das deutsche Lied: Probleme und Gestalten.* Hamburg, 1939.

"Die Lieder Beethovens: Eine stilkritische Studie," *Neues Beethoven Jahrbuch,* 2 (1925), 33–42.

Capell, Richard. *Schubert's Songs.* London, 1928. Reprint, 1957.

Cone, Edward. *The Composer's Voice.* Berkeley and Los Angeles, 1974.

Dahlhaus, Carl. *Nineteenth-Century Music,* trans. J. Bradford Robinson. Berkeley and Los Angeles, 1989.

Richard Wagner's Music Dramas, trans. Mary Whittall. Cambridge, 1979.

Damian, Franz Valentin. "Über das Lied 'Pause' aus Schuberts Liederkreis *Die schöne Müllerin,"* in *Schubert-Gabe der Oesterreichischen Gitarre-Zeitschrift,* 35–43. Vienna, 1928.

Dean, Winton. "Italian Opera" and "German Opera," in *The Age of Beethoven 1790–1830,* ed. Gerald Abraham. London, 1982, 376–522. Vol. VIII of *The New Oxford History of Music.*

Debryn, Carmen. *Vom Lied zum Kunstlied.* Göppingen, 1983.

Demmer, Sybille. *Untersuchungen zu Form und Geschichte des Monodramas.* Cologne and Vienna, 1982.

Deutsch, Otto Erich. "Schuberts zwei Liederhefte für Goethe," *Die Musik,* 21 (1928), 31–37.

Deutsch, Otto Erich, ed. *Schubert: Die Dokumente seines Lebens und Schaffens.* 3 vols. Munich, 1914. Enlarged edition, 1964, *Neue Ausgabe sämtlicher Werke,* series viii, vol. V; Eng. trans. 1946 as *Schubert: A Documentary Biography.* Reprint, 1977.

Schubert: Thematic Catalogue of all his Works in Chronological Order. London, 1951; Ger. trans., revised and enlarged, by Walther Dürr, Arnold Feil, Christa Landon, *et al.* as *Franz Schubert: thematisches Verzeichnis seiner Werke in chronologischer Folge von Otto Erich Deutsch.* Kassel, 1978.

Schubert: Die Erinnerungen seiner Freunde. Leipzig, 1957; 3rd edn., 1974; Eng. trans. 1958 as *Schubert: Memoirs by his Friends.*

Döhring, Sieghart. *Formgeschichte der Opernarie vom Ausgang des achtzehnten bis zur Mitte des neunzehnten Jahrhunderts.* Marburg, 1975.

Dräger, Hans Heinz. "Zur Frage des Wort–Ton-Verhältnisses in Hinblick auf Schuberts Strophenlied," *Archiv für Musikwissenschaft,* 11 (1954), 39–59.

"Schubert's Songs and Their Poetry: Reflections on Poetic Aspects of Song Composition," in *Schubert Studies: Problems of Style and Chronology,* ed. Eva Badura-Skoda and Peter Branscombe, 1–24. Cambridge, 1982.

Ebers, Gertraud. "Das Lied bei Haydn." Ph.D. diss., University of Innsbruck, 1943.

Eggebrecht, Hans Heinrich. "Prinzipien des Schubert-Liedes," *Archiv für Musikwissenschaft,* 27 (1970): 89–109.

Einstein, Alfred. *Mozart: His Character, His Work,* trans. Arthur Mendel and Nathan Broder. London, 1945.

Schubert: A Musical Portrait. New York, 1951.

Eliot, T. S. "The Three Voices of Poetry," in *On Poetry and Poets,* 96–112. New York, 1957.

Erk, Ludwig, and Franz M. Böhme. *Deutscher Liederhort.* 3 vols. Leipzig, 1893–94.

Fehn, Ann Clark, and Rufus Hallmark. "Text and Music in Schubert's Pentameter Lieder: A Consideration of Declamation," in *Music and Language,* 204–246. New York, 1983.

Bibliography

Feil, Arnold. *Franz Schubert: "Die schöne Müllerin," "Winterreise".* Stuttgart, 1975.

Fellinger, Imogen. *Verzeichnis der Musikzeitschriften des 19. Jahrhunderts.* Studien zur Musikgeschichte des 19. Jahrhunderts, vol. X. Regensburg, 1968.

Fischer-Dieskau, Dietrich. *Auf den Spuren der Schubert-Lieder: Werden, Wesung, Wirkung.* Wiesbaden, 1971; Eng. trans., 1976.

Fischer-Dieskau, Dietrich, comp. *The Fischer-Dieskau Book of Lieder,* trans. George Bird and Richard Stokes. New York, 1984.

Flesch, Siegried. Preface to *Orlando,* in *Hallische Händel-Ausgabe,* vol. XXVIII. Kassel, 1969.

Flössner, Franz. *Reichardt, der Hallische Komponist der Goethezeit.* Halle, 1929.

Flothuis, Marius. "Schubert Revises Schubert," in *Schubert Studies: Problems of Style and Chronology,* ed. Eva Badura-Skoda and Peter Branscombe, 61–84. Cambridge, 1982.

Friedländer, Max. *Das deutsche Lied im 18. Jahrhundert: Quellen und Studien.* 2 vols. Stuttgart and Berlin, 1902. Reprint, 1970.

Frisch, Walter, ed. *Schubert: Critical and Analytical Studies.* Lincoln, NE and London, 1986.

Frotscher, Gotthold. "Die Ästhetik des Berliner Liedes in ihren Hauptproblemen," *Zeitschrift für Musikwissenschaft,* 6 (1923–24), 431–448.

Georgiades, Thrasybulos. *Schubert: Musik und Lyrik.* Göttingen, 1967.

"'Das Wirtshaus' von Schubert und das Kyrie aus dem gregorianischen Requiem," in *Gegenwart im Geiste: Festschrift für Richard Benz,* ed. Walther Bulst and Arthur von Schneider, 126–135. Hamburg, 1954.

Goethe, Johann Wolfgang von. "Ballade, Betrachtung und Auslegung," in *Goethe: Gedichte,* ed. Erich Trunz, 400–402. Munich, 1981.

Der Briefwechsel zwischen Goethe und Zelter, ed. Max Hecker. 4 vols. Leipzig, 1913.

Der Briefwechsel zwischen Schiller und Goethe, ed. Hans Gerhard Gräf and Albert Leitzmann. 3 vols. Wiesbaden, 1955.

Faust: Eine Tragödie, 3rd edn. Deutscher Taschenbuch Verlag-Gesamtausgabe, vol. IX. Munich, 1966.

Goethe: Gedichte, ed. Erich Trunz. Munich, 1981.

Goethes Gespräche, ed. F. von Biedermann. 5 vols. Leipzig, 1909–11.

Goethe über seine Dichtungen, ed. Hans Gerhard Gräf. 9 vols. Frankfurt, 1901–14.

Goldschmidt, Hugo. "Traettas Leben und Werke," in *Denkmäler der Tonkunst in Bayern,* vol. XIV, no. 1. Leipzig, 1913.

Goslich, Siegfried. *Die deutsche romantische Oper.* Tutzing, 1975.

Gudewill, K. "Lied: A. Das Kunstlied im deutschen Sprachgebiet," *Die Musik in Geschichte und Gegenwart,* ed. Friedrich Blume. 14 vols. Kassel, 1949–68.

Hallmark, Rufus. "Schubert's 'Auf dem Strom,'" in *Schubert Studies: Problems of Style and Chronology,* ed. Eva Badura-Skoda and Peter Branscombe, 25–46. Cambridge, 1982.

Hamburger, Paul. "The Concert Arias," in *The Mozart Companion,* ed. H. C. Robbins Landon and Donald Mitchell, 324–360. London, 1956.

Haydn, Franz Joseph. *Joseph Haydn: Werke.* Series xxix: *Einstimmige Lieder,* ed. Joseph Haydn-Institut. Munich, 1958–.

Helm, Rudolf. *Skelett- und Todesdarstellungen bis zum Auftreten der Totentänze.* Strassburg, 1928.

Bibliography

Heuss, Alfred. "Eine Schubert-Liedstudie: Das Lied 'Pause' aus dem Zyklus *Die schöne Müllerin*," *Zeitschrift für Musik*, 91 (1924), 617–626.

Holmström, Kirsten Gram. *Monodrama, Attitudes, Tableaux Vivants: Studies of Some Trends of Theatrical Fashion 1770–1815*. Stockholm, 1967.

Istel, Edgar. *Die Entstehung des deutschen Melodramas*. Berlin and Leipzig, 1906.

Jander, Owen. "Beethoven's 'Orpheus in Hades': The *Andante con moto* of the Fourth Piano Concerto," *19th-Century Music*, 8/3 (1985), 195–212.

Kerman, Joseph. "A Romantic Detail in Schubert's *Schwanengesang*," *Musical Quarterly*, 48 (1962); 36–49.

Klein, Johannes. *Geschichte der deutschen Lyrik: Von Luther bis zum Ausgang des zweiten Weltkrieges*. Wiesbaden, 1957.

Krabbe, Wilhelm. "Das deutsche Lied im 17. und 18. Jahrhundert," in *Handbuch der Musikgeschichte*, ed. Guido Adler, vol. II, 691–703. 2 vols., Berlin, 1930.

Kramarz, Joachim. "Das Rezitativ im Liedschaffen Franz Schuberts." Ph.D. diss., Free University of Berlin, 1959.

Kramer, Lawrence. "Decadence and Desire: The *Wilhelm Meister* Songs of Wolf and Schubert," *19th-Century Music*, 10/3 (1987), 229–242.

Music and Poetry: The Nineteenth Century and After. Berkeley and Los Angeles, 1984.

"The Schubert Lied: Romantic Form and Romantic Consciousness," in *Schubert: Critical and Analytical Studies*, ed. Walter Frisch, 215–218. Lincoln, NE and London, 1986.

Kramer, Richard. "Schubert's Heine," *19th-Century Music*, 8 (1985), 213–225.

Krebs, Harald. "Techniques of Unification in Tonally Deviating Works," *Canadian University Music Review*, 10 (1990), 55–64.

"Tonart und Text in Schuberts Liedern mit abweichenden Schlüssen," *Archiv für Musikwissenschaft*, 47 (1990), 264–271.

Kretzschmar, Hermann. *Geschichte des neuen deutschen Liedes*, part 1. Kleine Handbücher der Musikgeschichte nach Gattungen, vol. IV. Leipzig, 1911. Reprint, 1966.

Kunze, Stefan. Introduction to *Bühnenwerke: Arien, Szenen, Ensembles und Chöre mit Orchester*, series ii, workgroup VII of *W. A. Mozart: Neue Ausgabe sämtlicher Werke*, ed. Ernst Fritz Schmid, Wolfgang Plath and Wolfgang Rehm. Kassel, 1955–.

"Die Vertonungen der Arie 'Non so d'onde viene' von J. Chr. Bach und W. A. Mozart," *Analecta musicologica*, 2 (1965), 85–111.

Landshoff, Ludwig. *Johann Rudolph Zumsteeg (1760–1802): Ein Beitrag zur Geschichte des Liedes und der Ballade*. Berlin, 1902.

Lewin, David. "'Auf dem Flusse': Image and Background in a Schubert Song," *19th-Century Music*, 6/1 (1982), 47–59.

Loewe, Karl. *Carl Loewes Werke: Gesamtausgabe der Balladen, Legenden, Lieder und Gesänge*, ed. M. Runze. 17 vols. Leipzig, 1899–1904. Facsimile edn., 1970.

Selbstbiographie, ed. Carl Hermann Bitter. Berlin, 1870.

Mackworth-Young, G. "Goethe's 'Prometheus' and Its Settings by Schubert and Wolf," *Proceedings of the Royal Musical Association*, 78 (1951–52), 53–65.

Maier, Gunter. *Die Lieder Johann Rudolf Zumsteegs und ihr Verhältnis zu Schubert*. Göppingen, 1971.

Bibliography

Mainka, Jürgen. "Das Liedschaffen Franz Schuberts in den Jahren 1815 und 1816: Schuberts Auseinandersetzung mit der Liedtradition des 18. Jahrhunderts." Ph.D. diss., Humboldt University, Berlin, 1958.

Manicke, Dietrich, ed. *Balladen von Gottfried August Bürger, in Musik gesetzt von André, Kunzen, Zumsteeg, Tomaschek und Reichardt*, vols. XLV–XLVI of *Das Erbe deutscher Musik*. Mainz, 1970.

Maschek, Hermann, and Hedwig Kraus, eds. *Das Wiener Lied von 1792 bis 1815*. Denkmäler der Tonkunst in Österreich, issue 42/2, vol. LXXIX. Reprint, 1960.

McKay, Elizabeth Norman. "Schubert as a Composer of Operas," in *Schubert Studies: Problems of Style and Chronology*, ed. Eva Badura-Skoda and Peter Branscombe, 85–104. Cambridge, 1982.

Mies, Paul. *Schubert, der Meister des Liedes: Die Entwicklung von Form und Inhalt im Schubertschen Lied*. Berlin, 1928.

Moser, Hans Joachim. "Carl Friedrich Zelter und das Lied," *Jahrbuch der Musikbibliothek Peters*, 39 (1932), 43–54.

Das deutsche Lied seit Mozart. 2 vols. Berlin and Zurich, 1937.

Das deutsche Sololied und die Ballade. Das Musikwerk, vols. XIV–XV. Cologne, 1957.

"Mozart als Liederkomponist," *Österreichische Musikzeitschrift*, 11 (1956), 90–94.

Mozart, Wolfgang Amadeus. *Briefe und Aufzeichnungen*, ed. Wilhelm A. Bauer and Otto Erich Deutsch. 7 vols. Kassel, 1962.

Wolfgang Amadeus Mozart: Neue Ausgabe sämtlicher Werke. Series ii, workgroup VII: *Arien, Szenen, Ensembles und Chöre mit Orchester*. Series iii, workgroup VIII: *Lieder mit Klavier und mit Mandoline*, ed. Ernst Fritz Schmid, Wolfgang Plath, and Wolfgang Rehm. Kassel, 1955–.

Mozart, Wolfgang, and Leopold Mozart. *Verzeichnis aller meiner Werke* and *Verzeichnis der Jugendwerke W. A. Mozarts*, ed. E. H. Mueller von Asow. Vienna and Wiesbaden, 1956.

Müller-Blattau, Joseph. "Händel," *Die Musik in Geschichte und Gegenwart*, ed. Friedrich Blume. 14 vols. Kassel, 1949–68.

Northcote, Sydney. *The Ballad in Music*. London, 1942.

Ossenkop, David Charles. "The Earliest Settings of German Ballads for Voice and Clavier." Ph.D. diss., Columbia University, 1968.

Pamer, Fritz Egon. "Das deutsche Lied im neunzehnten Jahrhundert," in *Handbuch der Musikgeschichte*, ed. Guido Adler, vol. II, 939–955. 2 vols., Berlin, 1930.

Pauli, Walther. *Johann Friedrich Reichardt: Sein Leben und seine Stellung in der Geschichte des deutschen Liedes*. Musikwissenschaftliche Studien, vol. II. Berlin, 1903.

Pestelli, Giorgio. "Opera Seria in the Second Half of the Eighteenth Century," in *The Age of Mozart and Beethoven*, 64–70. Cambridge, 1984.

Plantinga, Leon. *Romantic Music: A History of Musical Style in Nineteenth-Century Europe*. New York, 1984.

Pollak-Schlaffenberg, Irene. "Die Wiener Liedmusik von 1778–1789," *Studien zur Musikwissenschaft*, 5 (1918), 97–151.

Porter, Ernest G[raham]. *The Songs of Schubert*. London, 1937.

Schubert's Song Technique. London, 1961.

"Zumsteeg's Songs," *The Monthly Musical Record*, 88 (1958), 135–140.

Reed, John. *The Schubert Song Companion*. Manchester, 1985.

Bibliography

Reissmann, August. *Das deutsche Lied in seiner historischen Entwicklung.* Kassel, 1861.

Salmen, Walter. *Johann Friedrich Reichardt.* Freiburg, 1963.

Sams, Eric. "Lied," *The New Grove Dictionary of Music and Musicians*, ed. Stanley Sadie. London, 1980.

"Notes on a Magic Flute: The Origins of the Schubertian Lied," *The Musical Times*, 119 (1978), 947–949.

Sandberger, Adolf. "Johann Rudolph Zumsteeg und Franz Schubert," in *Ausgewählte Aufsätze zur Musikgeschichte*, 288–299. Munich, 1921.

Schauer, Hans, and Friedrich Wilhelm Wodtke. "Monodrama," in *Reallexikon der deutschen Literaturgeschichte*, vol. II, 415–418. Berlin, 1965.

Scheibler, Ludwig. "Franz Schuberts einstimmige Lieder, Gesänge und Balladen mit Texten von Schiller," *Die Rheinlande* (April–Sept. 1905), 131–136, 163–169, 231–239, 270–274, 311–315, 353–356.

Scherpe, Klaus R. *Gattungspoetik im 18. Jahrhundert: Historische Entwicklung von Gottschen bis Herder.* Stuttgart, 1968.

Schmitz, Eugen. *Geschichte der Kantate und des geistlichen Konzerts. I. Teil: Geschichte der weltlichen Solokantate.* Leipzig, 1914.

Schnapper, Edith. *Die Gesänge des jungen Schubert vor dem Durchbruch des romantischen Liedprinzips.* Berner Veröffentlichungen zur Musikforschung, vol. X. Bern and Leipzig, 1937.

Schochow, Maximilian, and Lilly Schochow, eds. *Franz Schubert: Die Texte seiner einstimmig komponierten Lieder und ihre Dichter.* Hildesheim and New York, 1974.

Schubert, Franz. *Franz Schubert: Neue Ausgabe sämtlicher Werke.* Series iv: *Lieder*, ed. Walther Dürr, Arnold Feil, *et al.* Kassel, 1964–.

Franz Schuberts Werke. Kritisch durchgesehene Gesamtausgabe, series xx: *Sämtliche einstimmige Lieder und Gesänge*, ed. Eusebius Mandyczewski, Johannes Brahms, *et al.* Leipzig, 1894–95. Reprint, 1964–69.

Schwab, Heinrich W[ilhelm]. *Sangbarkeit, Popularität und Kunstlied: Studien zu Lied und Liedästhetik der mittleren Goethezeit, 1770–1814.* Studien zur Musikgeschichte des neunzehnten Jahrhunderts, vol. III. Regensburg, 1965.

Schwarmath-Tarjan, Ermute. *Musikalischer Bau und Sprachvertonung in Schuberts Liedern.* Tutzing, 1969.

Spies, Günther. "Studien zum Liede Franz Schuberts: Vorgeschichte, Eigenart und Bedeutung der Strophenvariierung." Ph.D. diss., University of Tübingen, 1962.

Spitta, Philipp. "Die Ballade," in *Musikgeschichtliche Aufsätze*, 403–461. Berlin, 1894.

Staiger, Emil. *Grundbegriff der Poetik.* Zurich, 1946.

Stein, Deborah. "Schubert's Erlkönig: Motivic Parallelism and Motivic Transformation," *19th-Century Music*, 13/2 (1989), 145–158.

Stein, Franz A. *Verzeichnis deutscher Lieder seit Haydn.* Bern, 1967.

Stein, Jack M. *Poem and Music in the German Lied from Gluck to Hugo Wolf.* Cambridge, MA., 1971.

Sternfeld, Frederick W. *Goethe and Music: A List of Parodies and Goethe's Relationship to Music.* New York, 1954.

Stoljar, Margaret M. *Poetry and Song in Late Eighteenth Century Germany: A Study in the Musical Sturm und Drang.* London, 1985.

Strohm, Reinhard. *Die italienische Oper im 18. Jahrhundert.* Wilhelmshaven, 1979.

Szymichowski, Franz. "Johann Rudolph Zumsteeg als Komponist von Balladen und Monodien." Ph.D. diss., University of Frankfurt, 1932.

Bibliography

Thomas, J. H. "Schubert's Modified Strophic Songs with Particular Reference to *Schwanengesang*," *The Music Review*, 34 (1973), 83–99.

Weinrich, O. "Franz Schuberts Antikenlieder," *Deutsche Vierteljahresschrift für Literaturwissenschaft und Geistesgeschichte*, 13 (1935), 91–117.

Wigmore, Richard. *Schubert: The Complete Song Texts.* New York, 1988.

Wiora, Walter. *Das deutsche Lied: Zur Geschichte und Aesthetik einer musikalischen Gattung.* Wolfenbüttel and Zurich, 1971.

Wittmann, Gertraud. *Das klavierbegleitete Sololied Karl Friedrich Zelters.* Giessen, 1936.

Wolff, Christoph. "Schubert's 'Der Tod und das Mädchen': Analytical and Explanatory Notes on the Song D531 and the Quartet D810," in *Schubert Studies: Problems of Style and Chronology*, ed. Eva Badura-Skoda and Peter Branscombe, 143–171. Cambridge, 1982.

Youens, Susan. "Retracing a Winter Journey: Reflections on Schubert's *Winterreise*," *19th-Century Music*, 9 (1985), 128–135.

"Wegweiser in *Winterreise*," *The Journal of Musicology*, 5 (1987), 357–379.

Zelter, Carl Friedrich. *Carl Friedrich Zelter: 50 Lieder*, ed. Ludwig Landshoff. Mainz, 1932.

Carl Friedrich Zelter: 15 ausgewählte Lieder, ed. Moritz Bauer. Berlin, 1924.

Zumsteeg, Johann Rudolph. *Ausgewählte Lieder*, ed. Ludwig Landshoff. Berlin, 1902.

Kleine Balladen und Lieder in Auswahl, ed. Fritz Jöde. Nagels Musik-Archiv no. 82. Hannover, 1932.

INDEX

Index

Index

Index